W9-ACZ-909

YELLOW JACK

★

A HISTORY

BY SIDNEY HOWARD

IN COLLABORATION WITH PAUL DE KRUIF

★

DRAMATISTS
PLAY SERVICE
INC.

CARL A. RUDISILL
LIBRARY
LENOIR RHYNE COLLEGE

812
H 834
242 01

April, 1948

Copyright, 1933, 1934, by Sidney Howard

CAUTION: Professionals and amateurs are hereby warned that "Yellow Jack," being fully protected under the Copyright Laws of the United States of America, the British Empire, including the Dominion of Canada, and all other countries of the Copyright Union, is subject to royalty. All rights, including professional, amateur, motion picture, recitation, lecturing, public reading, radio broadcasting and the rights of translation into foreign languages are strictly reserved. Particular emphasis is laid on the question of readings, permission for which must be secured from the author's agent in writing. All inquiries except in connection with the amateur rights, should be addressed to the author's agent, Harold Freedman, 101 Park Avenue, New York City.

The nonprofessional acting rights of this play are controlled exclusively by the Dramatists Play Service, 6 East 39th Street, New York, N. Y., without whose permission in writing no performance of it may be made.

Full list of sound effect records and music is found on page iv.

17-943

43

... and suggestions on simplified staging, together with sugges-
... slight cuts and other modifications, enabling groups of high-
... age to produce the play.

YELLOW JACK has, since it was first produced, proved popular
and successful among little and community theaters, colleges and universities, and occasionally it has been used in whole or in part by high
schools and boys' prep schools. As originally produced, the play from
the stage appeared far simpler than when read in the printed text. The
author's note entitled " The Setting " (on page ix of the present text)
explains clearly just how it was produced in New York. The stage directions throughout refer to the original production. It has been produced in other ways, and one of its most successful productions was by
a group of boys in a prep school, under the direction of Mr. Donald
R. Towers at Lawrenceville School, Lawrenceville, New Jersey. Mr.
Towers made various suggestions to the Dramatists Play Service, some
of which are incorporated in the present notes. Mr. Towers, while
using the two levels, suggests that the second should be about $5\frac{1}{2}$ feet
high and about 12 feet deep. He adds that the screen in front of the
laboratory is not essential and unless it is well built and put on rollers,
may be a hindrance, since all changes have to take place in darkness.
He states also that steps in the center of the stage are helpful to the
action and adds finally that a cyclorama should be used.

Regarding the tents, he makes the suggestion that these be merely
skeletons and that scene shifts can be expedited by putting the tents
and cots on roller platforms.

It will be noted in the text that scenes are lighted in various parts
of the setting. This is a very simple thing to do, and it will be found
possible to change the furniture and props quite easily in those parts
of the stage that are not covered by a spot.

Music is used extensively throughout the play, and it is further
urged that it should be used invariably during shifts from one part of
the stage to another.

Of course, the singing and certain other sound effects can be produced by actual singing and homemade devices creating sound, but
phonograph records have proved very effective and we are appending
to this note a complete list of such records which can be furnished
through our office.

The director of this play is urged to use his own judgment in connection with scene shifts and the degree to which he wants to produce
a realistic scene or one that is suggestive and imaginative.

Although the play as written is definitely intended for production by
and for adults, we have received so many requests from high schools
and similar groups of young people that we have decided to make just
a few suggestions which we believe, if carried out, will enable any

iii

group of young people to do the play easily and without risking the kind of criticism which is found in some communities when young people use language which, though they may be accustomed to using it among themselves, they are not supposed to utter in public. There is a certain amount of swearing in this play and certain phrases which might in themselves be considered offensive, and though in our opinion all these should be spoken, nevertheless, they may be omitted without doing any very serious damage to the mood of the play.

There is just one feminine rôle in the play, that of the nurse, Miss Blake. Since this play is going to be used exclusively among groups of men and boys, it is suggested that Miss Blake can very easily be turned into a masculine character, and with practically no change in her lines.

SOUND EFFECTS AND MUSIC

Regarding the various singing that is indicated off-stage, it is possible that there are available and in stock certain records, but these we cannot undertake to supply. It is also feasible to have a vocal quartet off-stage sing either the songs indicated or similar, well-known old-timers. However, we can furnish sound effect records called for in the text as follows:

> No. 5028 Tom-tom off-stage.
> No. 5016 Bugle calls.
> No. 5017 (all requested).
> No. 5048 Sound of marching feet off-stage.
> No. 5029 Roll of drums.

The cost of each record is $2.20, which includes wrapping and carriage charges.

Sound for the shot off-stage can be indicated by record, but a somewhat better effect might result from using a real muffled shot or some good substitute.

LIST OF SUGGESTED VERBAL SUBSTITUTIONS

The following list is intended for the use in particular of groups of boys and young men in prep schools in those cases where the instructor considers that a few words and passages in this play may be deemed a bit "advanced" or possibly objectionable. YELLOW JACK is essentially a heroic drama in which men in all walks of life take their respective parts. The author in writing it has made use of certain words and expressions which are natural and proper in their places. It is urged that all groups using the play do their best to leave the text exactly as written, but we realize that in some cases this is not always advisable. Every such word or passage has been checked and indicated in the table that follows. In most cases we simply call attention to the word or words and suggest that either they be omitted or a milder substitute put in their place. The substituted word or phrase is not actually given.

PROPERTY LIST

(Depending on the kind of production that is planned, one may use many properties not absolutely essential, or few, most of which are actually used by the players. In connection with certain very small properties like the pipette and some of the small glass slides, these may be left to the imagination. The list below will undoubtedly prove sufficient for all practical purposes.)

Various flasks and test tubes for laboratory desks.
Mortar.
Pipette.
Rubber tubing.
Syringe and bottle of alcohol.
Towel.
Medical cotton.
Various typed papers.
Notebooks and pencils.
Typewriter.
Microscopes (2 to 5).
Bottle of whiskey, syphon, glasses.
Wire basket container with cotton plugged test tubes.
2 glass dishes for laboratory.
Several stretchers.
Slide boxes.

Culture flasks.
Bottles of stain.
3 or 4 printed or typed official documents.
Lantern.
2 books, one a college textbook.
Beer and 3 or 4 glasses.
Envelope with official paper.
Porcelain dish covered with gauze.
3 or 4 test tube racks.
Gauze-covered beakers.
Rifles for drilling soldiers.
Stethoscope.
Hypodermic needle.
U. S. bank note.
Pocket billfold.
File with patients' record cards.

Characters whose names appear in italics are inventions of the author to serve as substitutes for living participants in this story.

London: January, 1929

Stackpoole.
A Major of the Royal Air Force.
An Official of the Kenya Colony Government.
Two Laboratory Assistants.

West Africa: June, 1927

ADRIAN STOKES, of Guy's Hospital, London, attached to the West African Yellow Fever Commission, the Rockefeller Foundation.
Harkness, of the Rockefeller Commission.
Kraemer, of the same.
Chambang.

Cuba: Summer and Fall of 1900

WALTER REED, Major, M.C., U.S.A.
O'Hara
Brinkerhof ⎫ Privates,
McClelland ⎬ M.C., U.S.A.
Busch ⎭
Miss Blake, special nurse in charge of the Yellow Fever Ward.
Two Orderlies.
ARISTIDES AGRAMONTE ⎫ Assistant Surgeons, M.C., Members
JESSE W. LAZEAR ⎬ of the American Yellow Fever
JAMES CARROLL ⎭ Commission in Cuba.
WILLIAM CRAWFORD GORGAS, Major, M.C., U.S.A.
Colonel Jory, of the Marine Hospital Corps.
MAJOR CARTWRIGHT.
ROGER P. AMES, Assistant Surgeon, M.C., U.S.A.
CARLOS J. FINLAY, M.D.
WILLIAM H. DEAN, Private, U.S.A.
An Army Chaplain.
A Commissary Sergeant.
Soldiers.
Three Buglers.

West Africa: September, 1927

Harkness, of the West African Yellow Fever Commission, Rockefeller Foundation.

London: September, 1929

Stackpoole.

AN HISTORICAL PLAY which deals with events of recent times may well give offense to those characters in the play who are still alive. It is out of consideration for the survivors, therefore, that the authors have invented names for the characters still living.

But since the play is in part concerned with the deeds of four American soldiers, whose heroism should not go unrecorded, the true names of these soldiers are here given. They are: John J. Moran, John Kissenger, Warren Gladsden Jernegan, and Levi E. Folk.

Yellow Jack celebrates what these men did without attempting to portray them as they were.

THE SETTING

This play is written to be produced without conventional scenery upon a modern approximation of the Elizabethan stage. To facilitate the reader's understanding of the text, a description follows of the sculptural and noble setting designed by Jo Mielziner for the play's original production at the Martin Beck Theatre in New York.

The stage is divided into two levels, the upper lifted five feet above the floor of the stage and approached from below by twin flights of steps. These steps curve on either side of the central element of the upper level, a round bay which remains Reed's laboratory throughout the play. When the action does not utilize the laboratory, the bare equipment of which is arranged upon this central element, concealment is furnished by a semicircular wooden screen of lattice design to suggest a protection against the glare of tropic sunlight. This screen, of six leaves, divides in the center and rolls back on a circular track, so that when it is opened for the scenes in the laboratory it serves the actors as background. Properties or equipment for other laboratories, hospital beds, tents and other essentials, are mounted on low platforms which are pushed on at stage level through curtained arches to either side. A simple, flat arch masks the sky backdrop. The whole of the setting, including arch and floor, is covered with an unpainted khaki tan material.

The production uses nothing of realism beyond the properties which are absolutely essential to the action. Changes of locale are indicated only by alteration in the lighting. The action being continuous, the play flows in a constantly shifting rhythm of light.

The New York cast was as follows:

STACKPOOLE .... Geoffrey Kerr
AN OFFICIAL OF THE KENYA COLONY GOVERNMENT ...... Colin Hunter
A MAJOR OF THE ROYAL AIR FORCE .... Francis Compton
LABORATORY ASSISTANTS .... { Bernard Jukes / Lloyd Gough
KIM .... Kim
HARKNESS .... Robert Shayne
KRAEMER .... Wylie Adams
ADRIAN STOKES .... Charles Gerard
CHAMBANG .... Jack Carr
O'HARA .... James Stewart
MC CLELLAND .... Edward Acuff
BUSCH .... Samuel Levene
BRINKERHOF .... Myron McCormick
MISS BLAKE .... Katherine Wilson
ORDERLIES .... { Clyde Walters / Frank Stringfellow
WALTER REED .... John Miltern
JAMES CARROLL .... Barton MacLane
ARISTIDES AGRAMONTE .... Eduard Ciannelli
JESSE W. LAZEAR .... Robert Keith
COLONEL TORY .... Richie Ling
WILLIAM CRAWFORD GORGAS .... George Nash
MAJOR CARTWRIGHT .... Robert Shayne
ROGER P. AMES .... Harold Moffat
DR. CARLOS FINLAY .... Whitford Kane
WILLIAM H. DEAN .... Millard Mitchell
AN ARMY CHAPLAIN .... Lloyd Gough
A COMMISSARY SERGEANT .... Wylie Adams

YELLOW JACK

*The scene is London—*STACKPOOLE'S *laboratory, the time, January, 1929, and the sky is a London sky, a near sky, friendly for all its wintry grayness.*

A young laboratory assistant, slightly Cockney and GEORGE *by name, sits above on a stool at a bacteriological workbench in a bacteriological laboratory. He faces the audience over a line of flasks. He is at work on a combination of the liver of a monkey—lately dead of yellow fever—and sterile saline solution. His object is to transfer a minute amount of this commodity from the mortar in which he has prepared it to the Erlenmeyer flask in which, as he proposes, it will take its next step towards some desired result.* STACKPOOLE, *British, keen, aloof, distinguished and thirty-five, a* MAJOR *of the Royal Air Force and an* OFFICIAL *of the Kenya Colony government are grouped around the table watching* GEORGE *perform the experiment. The* MAJOR *is portly and florid in the British imperial manner. The* OFFICIAL *is an elderly and easily mannered gentleman and has a fine tropical sunburn.*

STACKPOOLE. That stuff he's grinding in the mortar is the pulp of a monkey's liver. A monkey that died this morning of yellow fever. Of course, the hope is that the liver's loaded with virus. The tricky thing about these monkeys, though—particularly with yellow fever—is the way the amount of virus in them varies. And the idea now is to test the degree of deadliness in this one.

MAJOR. I suppose that's a useful thing to know?

STACKPOOLE. When you're trying to get at a vaccine? Oh, yes, Major. Very.

OFFICIAL. How can you test the deadliness?

STACKPOOLE. That's simple enough. George is making a suspension of pulp in that first flask there. Then he'll dilute the suspension out weaker and weaker in each of those other flasks till he's arrived at the weakest dilution that will still be fatal. *(He points*

1

to the fifth flask in the row.) We have done the trick with as weak as one to a hundred thousand. But that was from a very high type of liver!

MAJOR. The trick? What trick, Dr. Stackpoole?

STACKPOOLE. Of killing another monkey! But this must seem very dry to you, gentlemen. You didn't come all this way to London to . . . Suppose we go down and get to your business. Any problem of the Colonial Airways interests me, Major. We won't disturb you, George? (STACKPOOLE, *the* MAJOR *and the* OFFICIAL *come down the stair.*)

GEORGE. No, sir.

STACKPOOLE. Sit down. Well, Major, so you don't like our quarantine regulations for air travel?

MAJOR. (*Pulling himself together.*) The men who built the British Empire weren't stopped by a tropical fever here and there! It's my job to develop new aviation projects. That's my notion of holding the Empire together. And you doctors and your confounded League of Nations are blocking me!

STACKPOOLE. (*Smiling.*) As bad as that?

MAJOR. Good God, I'm required to set up medical and pathological plants and maintain mosquito squads on every field I organize!

STACKPOOLE. Only in Africa!

MAJOR. I'm required to quarantine passengers for six days!

STACKPOOLE. Only passengers from the West Coast!

MAJOR. Do you expect passengers from anywhere to stand for that?

STACKPOOLE. (*Indicating* OFFICIAL.) Is my friend from Kenya Colony in sympathy with your protest?

OFFICIAL. I'm in favor of anything that keeps West Coast yellow fever on the West Coast where it belongs and away from the comparatively healthy people in my district.

MAJOR. Life's full of reasonable risks!

STACKPOOLE. Your planes are making yellow fever a bit too risky.

MAJOR. Rot, Dr. Stackpoole! I insist my . . .

STACKPOOLE. We're not in London, Major. We're on one of your African landing fields. (MAJOR *is puzzled.* STACKPOOLE *includes* OFFICIAL.) In Kenya Colony, say, in my old friend's district . . . (*Back to* MAJOR.) . . . where they haven't had yellow fever yet. And I'm just stepping out of one of your planes. A plane that's just brought me across from the West Coast, where I've caught

2

the disease. The merest beginnings of a case, you know. Might be malaria, might be a cold, might even be air pockets on the way. Well, I land, and a certain female mosquito bites me. Plenty of mosquitoes in Kenya Colony. Plenty of this particular mosquito. We'll call her the yellow fever mosquito, because she's especially equipped by an all-wise Providence to carry yellow fever from man to man. (*His tone becomes downright confidential.*) After she's bitten me—a few days after—she bites you. Or, perhaps, some fast traveling passenger bound north for the Sudan or south to Tanganyika or the Cape. Where plenty more of her agreeable species are waiting for their first meal of yellow fever blood. Has my fable answered your objections, Major?

MAJOR. (*Uncomfortably.*) There's always danger!

STACKPOOLE. You, with the British Empire on your mind! Think of India!

MAJOR. All right! I'm a good imperialist! I'll think of India!

STACKPOOLE. This mosquito's very much at home in India. Those steaming millions are still waiting for yellow fever. There's another point about India, too. The only animal ever found to be susceptible to the disease—except man, of course—is the common Indian monkey Stokes gave it to. Do you get the full beauty of the Indian picture? Monkeys and men both stricken together! Death in the village! Death falling from the treetops! And only one yellow fever passenger required to start the whole thing going! And every year your planes make the leap to India swifter and easier. It's a race between plague and science, isn't it? With your planes helping the plague to win. (*At this moment* GEORGE *in the eagerness of his work tips his stool too far forward and loses his balance. In doing this he breaks the pipette with which he is working.* STACKPOOLE *hears the noise and looks around.*) What is it, George?

GEORGE. Pipette broke! Cut through the glove!

STACKPOOLE. Let's see. (GEORGE *comes down to him.*) Get it off! (GEORGE *removes glove.*) Yes, by Jove!

GEORGE. (*Panic.*) I'll get it, doctor. I'll get it!

STACKPOOLE. There's no use carrying on about it. Sit down and take hold of yourself.

OFFICIAL. An accident?

MAJOR. Serious?

STACKPOOLE. He's cut himself on a pipette full of yellow fever virus. It's only a pin-prick, but . . . (*He calls.*) Mullins! (MUL-

3

LINS, *another laboratory assistant, enters.*) Clean up!

MULLINS. Crickey!

STACKPOOLE. Sit down, George.

MAJOR. Will he get yellow fever from that? }

OFFICIAL. I say, the poor devil! } (*Together.*)

STACKPOOLE. If you don't mind, gentlemen! (*To* GEORGE, *in good-humored irritability.*) Damn you, George. (*To* MULLINS.) Mullins!

MULLINS. Yes, sir?

STACKPOOLE. Get rubber tubing! (*He is rolling up his sleeve as* MULLINS *comes down to obey.*) Get a twenty c.c. syringe and alcohol. Draw up one c.c. of citrate salt solution. (*To* GEORGE.) Lend a hand, George. (GEORGE *fetches tubing and knots it around* STACKPOOLE'S *extended arm as* MULLINS *offers the syringe on a towel.*) Sterile?

MULLINS. Oh, yes, doctor. (STACKPOOLE *sits at desk, offering his arm to* MULLINS.)

STACKPOOLE. Well, go ahead! There's the vein. What are you waiting for? (MULLINS, *after proper swabbing with alcohol, inserts the needle into the vein.*) Fill her right up. (*To* GEORGE.) Take off your coat. (*Back to* MULLINS.) Right.

MULLINS. Centrifuge, doctor?

STACKPOOLE. Quicker we get it into him the better. (*Indicating* GEORGE.) Pull up his shirt. (MULLINS *pulls* GEORGE'S *shirt out of his trousers, baring his back.*) Right. (*He makes injection.* GEORGE *winces.* MAJOR *and* OFFICIAL *turn aside.*) No good worrying, George. We've done what we could. (*To* MULLINS.) Better take him home.

GEORGE. I can carry on, sir.

STACKPOOLE. Take him out of here. Buy him a drink. (*The two assistants go,* STACKPOOLE *watching them as he restores his shirt sleeve to order. He puts on his coat and rubs alcohol on his hands, then smiles at his guests in apologetic explanation.*) Sorry, gentlemen. When we take a glass rod and rub a drop of that virus on a monkey's belly, on the unbroken skin, the monkey dies. So you see, an actual cut . . .

OFFICIAL. Will he be all right?

STACKPOOLE. If he were a monkey he would. . . . I don't know that that's ever been done before . . . to a man.

MAJOR. Blood transfusion?

STACKPOOLE. (*Amused.*) No, Major. I'm lending him some of my

4

immunity, that's all. I hope it serves. He's a good assistant.

OFFICIAL. Have you had yellow fever? (STACKPOOLE *nods casually.*)

MAJOR. In Africa?

STACKPOOLE. No. I caught it right here in the lab.

MAJOR. I think I'll sit down again. I feel a bit unsteady. (*He sits.*)

STACKPOOLE. Drink?

MAJOR. No, thanks.

STACKPOOLE. We'll all sit down and go on where we left off. (*He motions* OFFICIAL *to a chair.*)

MAJOR. I'm not sure I can get back to the subject.

OFFICIAL. The Major's here in London working out the new flight schedule to India. Cutting the time considerably, you know. . . . (*A side glance at* MAJOR.) With stop-overs in Cairo to connect with yellow fever.

STACKPOOLE. (*Stern.*) How long will you take from the West Coast of Africa to India? Don't cut that down too much.

MAJOR. We can't hold progress back for you science fellows!

(*The scene becomes angry.*)

STACKPOOLE. Don't think we're not doing what we can! In West Africa, in Brazil, in New York and Boston! I've been at it here for the past . . .

MAJOR. What's holding you back?

STACKPOOLE. It isn't easy to work with a microbe you can't see!

MAJOR. But with your microscopes . . .

STACKPOOLE. Not with any microscope ever made!

MAJOR. Ah, but you can't see smallpox, either! And if you can vaccinate against that . . .

STACKPOOLE. I'm working on a vaccine for this.

MAJOR. Use it!

STACKPOOLE. I don't dare yet. What protects a monkey might kill a man.

MAJOR. Get after your mosquito then!

STACKPOOLE. Will you pay for the oil to cover equatorial Africa?

MAJOR. Well, for God's sake, get your vaccine in time!

STACKPOOLE. In time, Major! Knowledge won't be hurried! They'd been working a hundred and some years at this when that solid American citizen, Walter Reed, found the yellow fever mosquito in Havana. In 1900 that was. Had to experiment on human beings to find it. Didn't have any laboratory animal then that would

5

take the disease. Quite a yarn that. Should have gone quickly on to a general festival of vaccination! But for eighteen years Germans and Frenchmen, Britishers and Brazilians sweated in tropical jungles and fever towns to finish Reed's work and got nowhere, till the little Jap Noguchi announced he'd discovered the microbe in Ecuador. Only Noguchi turned out to be wrong. That's a yarn, too. And the thing stuck there, still for want of a laboratory animal. Human beings aren't practical for experiment. Men of Reed's "thoroughness" don't happen often. That may be just as well. Then in the summer of 1927 Stokes succeeded at last in giving the disease to his Indian monkey. Gave us an animal we could experiment on. Put the thing in our labs where we could get at it! Started us after a vaccine in earnest! But the disease turned on us workers then. Killed Stokes in his laboratory in West Africa. Killed Noguchi. Killed and will kill plenty more of us. The whole thing's a yarn, looking back on it. A thirty-year long detective serial. And the best any of us can hope for is to get his own installment written and fitted in. How many more installments? I wish I knew! I'm afraid you'll have to stick to your quarantines, Major. (*A pause.* MAJOR *rises, disgruntled.*)

MAJOR. I can't say you've helped my problem, Dr. Stackpoole. Nor increased my respect for medical science, either.

STACKPOOLE. (*Laughing.*) Now, don't despair of science, Major! We never do! Never wake up in the morning without saying: "Today may be the day for the lucky accident!"

MAJOR. I shall have to blunder on as best I can. (MAJOR *is going.*)

STACKPOOLE. Come back in a year! We might have something to show you!

OFFICIAL. You did say just what I wanted of you. I hope we haven't taken too much of your time. (*They shake hands.*)

STACKPOOLE. Not at all! Not at all! Good-bye. (OFFICIAL *goes.* STACKPOOLE *stands thoughtful for a moment, glances at his calendar, then, solo.*) The twelfth. Four days. If George gets through the sixteenth all right . . . (*He shrugs, glances at his watch, and calls.*) Mullins!

MULLINS. (*Off-stage.*) Yes, sir?

STACKPOOLE. Is Kim ready?

MULLINS. (*Off-stage.*) Ready, sir. (*He enters, carrying under his arm a small Scottish terrier pup.*)

STACKPOOLE. How's George feeling?

MULLINS. Oh, he's all right, sir. A bit shaky, you know.

6

STACKPOOLE. I'm that myself. I shall walk Kim over.

MULLINS. If anyone asks for you, sir?

STACKPOOLE. I'm only going to Dr. Laidlaw's. I shan't be long. (*Then, to the dog.*) Are you ready, Kim? (*Kim is ready.*) Good. Yellow fever may have us stumped, but we *can* vaccinate you against distemper. (*He stops in his tracks. Then, so absently.*) Think you could put your finger on those notes Laidlaw and Dunkin sent over? About their vaccine for dog distemper?

MULLINS. (*Extracting typed papers from the desk drawer.*) Right here, sir.

STACKPOOLE. Thanks. Take Kim. George! (MULLINS *takes the pup.* GEORGE *enters.* STACKPOOLE *drops papers on desk and stands looking down on them.*) " Dogs of known susceptibility to distemper are taken and a small but certainly infective dose of living virus is injected into each. This is followed by an appropriate injection of immune blood serum. The results of this *combined* dosage of *both* living virus and immune serum have been in every case highly satisfactory and *solid immunity* to later doses of living virus has been demonstrated in every animal." (*He looks up.*) More or less what just happened to you, George. Virus plus a shot of immune blood. Only we'll have to be neater about things than you were. At least control the amount of virus. Still, if you pull through . . . (*He looks down at Kim.*) The principle does seem to work for Kim. . . . (*Then, very low.*) Why shouldn't it work for . . . (*He stops embarrassed. Then:*) Thanks, Kim. (*He leans over to pat Kim's head.*) Thanks for the suggestion. (*To* MULLINS.) You walk Kim over. He's earned a walk and I'm not going out. (*His whole manner sharpens as* MULLINS *leads Kim out.*) Any other monkeys die last night, George?

GEORGE. There's one that's pretty near gone, Dr. Stackpoole.

STACKPOOLE. (*Very deliberate.*) We'll get the living virus out of him and the immune blood serum out of me and if Laidlaw's principle can be applied . . .

GEORGE. (*Kindling.*) Yes, sir! Right, sir!

STACKPOOLE. I'll want four healthy monkeys. Stokes's Indian monkeys. You pick 'em out for me, George.

GEORGE. Trust me, sir.

STACKPOOLE. We'll vaccinate one pair with Laidlaw's combination and shoot living virus into the others straight. They'll die, that second pair, but the first pair . . . (*He sits at his desk making notes.*)

GEORGE. They'll be all right, sir! They'll be as well as . . .

STACKPOOLE. Go slow, George! Been fooled so many times! It would be a step in the right direction, though.

GEORGE. Yes, sir. (*He goes.*)

STACKPOOLE. What's the date? (*A glance at calendar.*) January 12th, 1929. (*He is writing. Slowly the light concentrates upon him until only his head and shoulders are visible.*) Reasonable hope . . . experiments initiated herewith . . . establish at least principle of vaccination against yellow fever. . . . Following the discovery made eighteen months ago in West Africa . . . (*In the distance a tom-tom is faintly audible.*) by the late Dr. Adrian Stokes . . . of the susceptibility of the Indian Rhesus monkey . . . (HARKNESS'S *voice interrupts from the darkness.*)

HARKNESS. "This recommendation is based upon a record of failure . . ." (*The click of a portable typewriter is audible through the beat of the tom-tom, then light shows another laboratory workbench, far less complete in equipment than its predecessors. It displays little more than the microscope, the typewriter itself and a bottle of whiskey with syphon and glasses.* HARKNESS, *a young American adventurer in medical science, sits on a stool. He is clad in soiled summer linen slacks and shirtsleeves and his mood is sour as he operates the typewriter to transcribe from a longhand draft which he has to hand.*) ". . . a failure so consistent . . . as to offer no encouragement to continuing the present research here in West Africa." (*He mops his brow.*) " The animals which we have attempted to infect with yellow fever blood include . . . rabbits, white mice, African and South American monkeys . . . puppies, kittens, goats . . . and over a thousand European and American guinea pigs." (*Another swallow of his drink.*) " In no instance during the entire nine months has any animal shown the least reaction to the disease. Nor does the enthusiasm of Dr. Stokes hold any promise of . . ."

(KRAEMER *enters above. He is another young American similarly dressed except that he wears a pith helmet. He carries a wire basket container filled with cotton-plugged test tubes and packed with small pieces of ice.*)

KRAEMER. You still up, Harkness?

HARKNESS. Where did you come from?

KRAEMER. Those native villages up behind Suhum. Waited for dark to drive in. Thought it might be cooler. It wasn't.

HARKNESS. New cases?

KRAEMER. Plenty. (*He sets wire basket on table.* HARKNESS *turns to sweeten his drink.*)

HARKNESS. What's that?

KRAEMER. Didn't hear anything.

HARKNESS. Sounded like somebody whooping.

KRAEMER. Natives.

HARKNESS. Didn't sound like natives.

KRAEMER. Not Stokes!

HARKNESS. What would Stokes have to whoop about?

KRAEMER. Can't imagine. Can't tell about the Irish, though.

HARKNESS. Don't hear anything now.

KRAEMER. You're cracking up.

HARKNESS. Just two white men going to hell in the tropics. (*A sip of his drink.*) Better make yourself one.

KRAEMER. I've got a day's work to do tomorrow. . . . So have you. (*The scene becomes quick with stubborn anger.*)

HARKNESS. I don't need to be reminded of that, Kraemer.

KRAEMER. Where do you want these bloods?

HARKNESS. Don't leave 'em there. The damn ice will melt and mess everything up.

KRAEMER. Aren't you going to inject the animals?

HARKNESS. Why should I?

KRAEMER. I drove eighty miles and got stuck twice and changed a flat in this heat to get those bloods here.

HARKNESS. Put 'em in the icebox. I'll go through the motions in the morning. I'm turning in now.

KRAEMER. They won't be fresh in the morning.

HARKNESS. What difference will that make?

KRAEMER. All right! I'll go down and inject 'em myself!

HARKNESS. Go ahead. (*He is gathering up coat, cigarettes and whiskey bottle.*) There's a whole new generation of guinea pigs and you can help yourself to Stokes's imported monkeys. I'm fed up. If you don't know we're wasting time here you're a bloody fool.

KRAEMER. (*Low.*) I'm not wasting time!

HARKNESS. On a disease you can't give to any animal but man?

KRAEMER. I don't believe that yet.

HARKNESS. How can we get anywhere with no animal to experiment on!

KRAEMER. We may find one yet.

9

HARKNESS. (*Turning savagely.*) Want to know where to look for your animal? I'll tell you! I'll tell you the only place! Go down to the village and shanghai some natives. You'll get nowhere with this any other way.

KRAEMER. Oh, Harkness, for the love of . . .

HARKNESS. What the hell! Reed and his gang did that in Cuba! (*The idea fascinates him.*) I walked through the village this afternoon and saw 'em. If these planes turn out the menace people say . . .

KRAEMER. Don't talk like a fool! (*He sits wearily.*)

HARKNESS. I'm sorry, Kraemer. I'll go down and inject the animals, of course. You go to bed. (*He is picking up container.*)

KRAEMER. (*Peacemaker.*) We'll get out of here sometime, Harkness. Where we won't have to shoot quinine every day. It's hard to believe, but we will. (ADRIAN STOKES *enters quickly above. He is an Irishman, aged forty. At the moment his hair is tousled and he wears thoroughly mussed pajamas. He carries four microscope slides on a board. He is followed by* CHAMBANG, *a stalwart African negro in shorts, shoes and nothing else.* CHAMBANG *carries two glass dishes in which some bloody mess is dimly visible.*) Hello there, Stokes! (STOKES *has come down to workbench and set himself to the adjustment of the microscope.* CHAMBANG *places glass dishes before him and stands easily at attention.* STOKES *works in intense concentration, his eyes shining.* KRAEMER *has decided on a drink after all and is reaching for the bottle as he continues easily.*) What got you out of bed? Harkness thought he heard you whooping a while back.

STOKES. Likely he did.

HARKNESS. Just lying in bed whooping himself to sleep.

STOKES. I wasn't in bed.

HARKNESS. Where were you?

STOKES. I was down in the monkey house. (*The slightest pause, then:*)

KRAEMER. What for?

CHAMBANG. (*Grinning.*) Number Eleven. He is dead, Dr. Kraemer.

HARKNESS. Dead? Number Eleven?

CHAMBANG. Surely not unexpected, Dr. Harkness, in view of **fever** this afternoon.

HARKNESS. He was all over his cage before supper!

STOKES. (*Indicating dishes in turn.*) If it's evidence of his death you want, that's liver there and those are his kidneys.

KRAEMER. (*Breathless.*) My God, have you cut him up already? (*And he is on his knees to examine the liver dish.*)

STOKES. He wasn't wearing his liver around his neck.

HARKNESS. Don't get too cocky, Stokes. Monkeys do die of all kinds of things besides yellow fever.

STOKES. Have I made any assertion? I say only this: that monk was injected with yellow fever blood eight days ago. Blood from Christian Otumanko, black, and Kwasi Danso, even blacker. Mild native cases, up and about already. But the monkey's dead, Harkness! Fever this afternoon! Dead as a mackerel now! Dead, Holy God Almighty! (*Even* HARKNESS *is shaken with the impact of this, but* KRAEMER *looks up from liver at which he has been peering.*)

KRAEMER. Hey! Look! (HARKNESS *looks, then:*)

HARKNESS. Well, something certainly hit that liver!

KRAEMER. I haven't seen a liver like that since . . .

HARKNESS. Since that dead Syrian we had last March at Lagos!

KRAEMER. The rug man!

HARKNESS. Right!

STOKES. The eyes were a disappointment to me, showing little or no yellow at all. But the kidneys are a beautiful color. (HARKNESS *turns to look at kidneys.* STOKES'S *slide is prepared.*) Shall we look at the liver section now? (KRAEMER *springs to his feet and* HARKNESS, *too, moves suddenly, but they both remember in the nick of time that this is primarily* STOKES'S *moment.*)

KRAEMER. (*A gulp, then:*) Go ahead. (*In the distance the tom-tom resumes its throb.* STOKES *looks long and carefully while* KRAEMER *watches, holding his breath. Then he rises and motions to* KRAEMER *to take his place. He stands back, his chest swelling, his smile broadening.* HARKNESS *looks up as* KRAEMER *sits and looks.* KRAEMER *surrenders his place to* HARKNESS, *who looks in turn quickly, then lifts his head.*)

HARKNESS. My God! (*He gets to his feet and moves giddily away from the miracle and* STOKES *is quickly back in his place for a second look.* HARKNESS *can hardly speak for his excitement.*) I'm sold. Those liver cells are enough for me. (*Then, with good-humored irritability:*) Damn you, Stokes!

KRAEMER. Yes, and you only just off the boat from London!

HARKNESS. And we wasting months trying every monk in Africa! And here you come with your damn Indian monk . . .

KRAEMER. That's where Stokes was smarter than . . .

HARKNESS. You've done it, Stokes! By God, I hand it to you! A

11

disease that's been a closed book all these years! A disease we've known only from its human victims! And here you've found us an animal at last! And put the thing where we . . .

KRAEMER. (*Wild.*) Twenty-five, twenty-seven years they've all been looking! Ever since Reed's experiments on the soldiers!

HARKNESS. Longer than that! Do you think Reed didn't look before he . . .

KRAEMER. No more human experiment now that Stokes has done it! (STOKES *sits smiling but quite calm as he examines the other three slides on his board.*)

STOKES. Done it, you say?

KRAEMER. Yes, that's what I said.

STOKES. But we haven't even started.

HARKNESS. I'm satisfied. We can get after the vaccine now!

STOKES. (*Working.*) I'm not satisfied. Chambang, fetch me another monk.

HARKNESS. Wait a minute, Chambang! (*To* STOKES.) What for?

STOKES. (*Working.*) The first thing's to keep this strain alive and going from monkey to monkey till . . .

KRAEMER. We've only got three monks left.

STOKES. This one took eight days dying. At that rate three more should allow us twenty-four days to get others from Hamburg. Kraemer, send Karl Hagenbeck a cable! Tell him you want all the Rhesus monkeys he's got on hand! And he'd better get more from India!

HARKNESS. Monkeys cost money!

STOKES. Five hundred monkeys are cheaper than one man! Can we begin to think of a vaccine till we've seen dozens of monks die as this one's died? Till we've exhausted every possible test? We'll have the whole world firing questions at us!

KRAEMER. Questions?

HARKNESS. (*At the same time.*) After this?

STOKES. (*Scorn.*) This? What is this? A monk's dead of a fever out of a black man's blood! A fever mild among African natives. Will they agree out there that this is the real old murdering yellow jack! Do *we* know that it is?

CHAMBANG. (*Quietly, from above.*) Black man little fever. White man big fever. White man die.

STOKES. Chambang's said it! I'll not be satisfied till I've seen dead white man and dead monk side by side on the autopsy table!

HARKNESS. Jesus!

12

STOKES. Fetch me another monk, Chambang! (CHAMBANG *goes above*.) There's an epic of work for us to be doing now, for I'll believe nothing till I can't help myself! (*He is back at his work again*.)

KRAEMER. (*Quiet and smiling*.) Well, it may be years, but it must come now.

HARKNESS. Walter Reed once said those very words!

STOKES. Walter Reed!

KRAEMER. Wonder what they'll say in New York tomorrow?

STOKES. I'd rather think of what Walter Reed would have said . . . (*In the distance a* QUARTET *is heard singing very faintly*.)

QUARTET. "When you hear dem bells go ding-a-ling . . ."

BASS. "Boom. Boom. Boom."

STOKES. (*Continuing over the singing*.) And of what Lazear and Carroll would have said . . .

QUARTET. (*A little louder*.) "All join round and a-sweetly you must sing . . ."

BASS. "And when the . . ."

STOKES. (*Over the singing*.) Yes, and the soldiers back there in Havana in 1900. What would they say to . . . (*Darkness*.)

QUARTET. (*Full volume*.)

> " Verse am over, in the chorus all join in :
>   There'll be a hot time in the old town tonight! "

BASS. "My baby . . ." (*Through the darkness* QUARTET *repeats full volume. Then the scene is Columbia Barracks at Quemado, near Havana, Cuba. The time is late July, 1900. A line of American* SOLDIERS *is crossing the stage. It walks through shadow, in tragic single file, each pair of* SOLDIERS *carrying a stretcher. On each stretcher is a dummy corpse covered with an army blanket. The refrain is repeated as the scene is revealed*.)

QUARTET. (*Continuing*.)

> " Good-bye, Dolly, I must leave you,
>   Though it breaks my heart to go;
> Something tells me I am wanted
>   At the front, to fight the foe,
> See, the soldier boys are marching
>   And I can no longer stay,

13

Hark, I hear the bugles calling,
Good-bye, Dolly Gray!"

(*And then continuing from "Dolly Gray.*")

"Good-bye, my Blue Bell,
Farewell to you!
One last fond look into
Your eyes of blue.
'Mid campfires' gleaming
'Mid shot and shell,
I will be dreaming
Of my own Blue Bell!"

(*Then, as the last stretcher passes, "There'll Be a Hot Time in the Old Town Tonight" is repeated diminuendo. Four American* SOLDIERS, *all of whom wear the Medical Corps insignia, are fixedly watching the passage of the stretchers. These four are, by name,* O'HARA, BRINKERHOF, MC CLELLAND *and* BUSCH. O'HARA *is a husky young Irishman of spirit and intelligence, his speech still stiff with the brogue of Galway.* BRINKERHOF *is an Ohio Valley boy, gentle, serious and soft-spoken.* BUSCH *is a city chap of Jewish extraction and intensity.* MC CLELLAND, *a Southerner, is the sturdy and commonplace member of the group. All four are still in their earliest twenties and because they are all dressed alike should be cast with due consideration for variety of personal type. The singing comes to a halt. The last of the stretchers passes.* O'HARA *makes the sign of the cross.*)

O'HARA. Pray God that may be the last of them for this day!
MC CLELLAND. (*Shuddering.*) This medical corps's a bad disappointment to me! Drill and tote stretchers! Swab out the ambulance! Swab out the latrine! I don't like the smell of chlorine and carbolic! Sickness and dying ain't congenial to my nature! And all the time waiting for my turn to go out feet first! The war's over! Why don't they send us home?
BUSCH. (*Indignant.*) Ain't you heard how they're making the Caribbean an American lake? Uncle Sam's going to keep us right here in Cuba till the natives have all learned to call him daddy! Or anyway till they quit calling him a thief! We're pawns, that's all, in the game of imperialism! I get my ideas out of reading Karl Marx.

BRINKERHOF. (*Blandly.*) One man's meat is another man's poison, as the saying goes. I think Cuba's a real Paradise on earth. It don't matter how hot the days get there's always a cool breeze at night. I got to admit yellow jack's a drawback. But even so, this life's a lot better than what I used to have in Liberty Mills, Indiana, where I come from.

O'HARA. (*Blarney.*) 'Tis a fine, easy land, as John Brinkerhof says and the tropical climate offers advantages over the rainy coast of Ireland where I was born. As to yellow jack, such afflictions are questions of fate and it behooves us to be philosophers where fate is concerned which the Irish are so long as their fate remains agreeable.

MC CLELLAND. I'd sooner be home than here, raising a family and living a normal life.

BUSCH. And me! I'd sooner be back in Chicago where I belong, furthering the interests of the radical movement.

BRINKERHOF. I'll bide my time here till I get my sergeancy.

O'HARA. A future of noble medical ambition stretches out before Johnny O'Hara like a green meadow ablossom with the sufferings of his fellow men. I'll never be satisfied till I'm Dr. O'Hara!

(MISS BLAKE [1] *enters. She is a trained nurse, Southern, lean and in her thirties.*)

MISS BLAKE. Will you tell the Major, please, Mr. Brinkerhof, that the patient he was interested in has just died? (*Extreme solemnity descends on the four soldiers.*)

O'HARA. Died, is it?

MC CLELLAND. One of our boys?

BUSCH. Was it yellow jack?

BRINKERHOF. Major Reed's right here in his laboratory, Miss Blake, waiting for Dr. Carroll to come back from Pinar del Rio.

MISS BLAKE. Then I'll go tell him myself. (*But two* ORDERLIES *enter carrying a stretcher covered with a blanket. They pass below the* SOLDIERS, *who look on hypnotized as* MISS BLAKE *goes towards where light grows on the laboratory of the American Yellow Fever Commission in Cuba. The laboratory furnishings consist of a workbench upon which the now antiquated brass microscopes stand amidst a litter of slides, slide boxes and notebooks. Stools and some shelves filled with culture flasks, bottles of stain and other specimens of laboratory glassware complete the*

[1] See note on p. iv.

equipment. WALTER REED, *Major M.C.—slim, distinguished, Virginian, fifty—sits at the workbench in the meanwhile.*)

1ST ORDERLY. Go easy, there!

2ND ORDERLY. Let me get hold!

1ST ORDERLY. Hands slipping?

2ND ORDERLY. Jesus, it's hot! I'm sweating. (*The stretcher is set down while he mops his brow.*) Hope they get the door of that autopsy room unlocked and don't keep us waiting where everybody can see. (*The stretcher resumes its course.*)

1ST ORDERLY. Straight ahead. (*They are going.* REED *looks up from the papers* MISS BLAKE *has handed him.*)

REED. Name: John Davies. Age: twenty-two. He wasn't married. That's always some consolation. I must write to his mother.

MISS BLAKE. Yes, doctor.

BRINKERHOF. I knew that boy. He come from Indiana near where I come from. I was pitching horseshoes with him last Friday. (*He turns sorrowfully apart.*) Now he's dead.

REED. (*Calling.*) Brinkerhof! (BRINKERHOF *goes up into laboratory and salutes.*)

MC CLELLAND. This Cuba's a hell of a place to spend the summer.

REED. (*To* BRINKERHOF.) Get word to Dr. Agramonte that there's a subject for him in the autopsy room. Say I'll join him there. (BRINKERHOF *salutes and goes.* REED *buries his head in his hands.*) That's all, Miss Blake. (MISS BLAKE *hesitates an instant, then turns out of laboratory and comes down towards the* SOLDIERS. *In the meanwhile:*)

BUSCH. (*A fearful whisper to* O'HARA.) O'Hara!

O'HARA. What?

BUSCH. Will they cut him up now?

O'HARA. In the lofty hope of finding a microbe in him!

MC CLELLAND. (*Sickened.*) Will you lay off that medical talk!

O'HARA. If I had the disease myself I'd take comfort in offering my remains to the service of science and not waste them buried whole beneath grass or marble!

BUSCH. Why couldn't these lousy docs of cured him?

MISS BLAKE. That's no way to speak of the doctors, Mr. Busch!

BUSCH. What kind of doctors are they? Do they think us boys enlisted and come down here so they can cut us up and squint at our insides?

MC CLELLAND. The doctors kind of give me a pain, too. And in front of you, Miss Blake, I wouldn't say where.

16

BUSCH. (*To* MISS BLAKE.) You know yellow jack when you see it, don't you?

MISS BLAKE. I ought to by this time.

BUSCH. You don't think any of us got it? You don't think I got it? I bet I got it!

MC CLELLAND. He looks yellow to me!

MISS BLAKE. That's not funny!

BUSCH. No, it ain't! All this week I been feeling terrible and my food don't set right and I can't keep my mind on Karl Marx!

MC CLELLAND. That's what give it to him! Karl Marx give it to him!

O'HARA. The way sitting on a cold stone gives a man piles!

MISS BLAKE. Be quiet, you two!

BUSCH. I can't eat! By rights I ought to eat to keep up my strength! I can't get no strength out of my food! It don't stay with me long enough!

MISS BLAKE. Put out your tongue. (*He obeys.* O'HARA *and* MC CLELLAND *strain to watch the examination, grinning.*) How long did you say you'd been feeling badly?

BUSCH. Oh, God, I have got it! (O'HARA *and* MC CLELLAND *recoil.* BRINKERHOF *looks up.*)

MISS BLAKE. Castor oil will cure any yellow fever you've got.

BUSCH. Oh, no, Miss Blake! Things is bad enough with me that way already! I bet I got it! I bet I'm a stiff before I know it!

O'HARA. Oh, he's as good as on the autopsy table already!

MISS BLAKE. Are you trying to scare the boy to death?

BUSCH. He don't have to try! I ain't ashamed I'm scared of this! I'll take on any man twice my weight! I may be Jewish but I got guts! Would I be a radical if I didn't have? Put me up against anything and I'll show you! (*Then he adds:*) Only it's got to be something I can see.

MISS BLAKE. A disease like this wants a special courage, Mr. Busch.

O'HARA. It wants the noble variety that's in us medical men the way we can live in the midst of a dreadful plague with no effect on the gayety of our spirits! When I see Major Reed and his men of science how they expose themselves to the perils of this, worrying after the unknown truth of it like a bevy of bulldogs, glory be to God, I . . . (*During these remarks* REED *has risen wearily and come out of the laboratory just in time to hear his name.* MC CLELLAND *sees him.*)

17

MC CLELLAND. 'TenSHUN!

BUSCH. (*Under his breath.*) Jesus! (*The four boys are statues. A low exclamation of dismay from* MISS BLAKE, *then.*)

REED. Hadn't you better get back to your ward, Miss Blake?

MISS BLAKE. Yes, doctor. Perhaps I had. (*She goes.* AGRAMONTE *enters above carrying a dish, presumably of tissue from the autopsy just performed. He proceeds at once to prepare his slide for microscopic examination. In the meanwhile* REED *has turned to* BUSCH.)

REED. What's your name?

BUSCH. Busch. Levi P., sir. Private, Quartermaster Department.

(REED *turns inquiringly to* MC CLELLAND.)

REED. And yours?

MC CLELLAND. McClelland. Warren G., sir. Private, Transportation Unit. (REED *turns to* O'HARA.)

O'HARA. O'Hara. John J., sir. Acting sergeant in charge of the operating room, sir.

REED. Oh, you're the one who wants to be a doctor!

O'HARA. I am that, sir, and progressing nicely thanks to the doctors the way they allow me opportunities to observe surgery and even administer the anesthetic, as I have done on three separate occasions due to my natural aptitude for the healing arts. (REED *smiles.*)

REED. I think you've kissed the Blarney stone in your day.

O'HARA. I was born where the eloquent tongue is native, sir.

(" *Retreat* " *is sounding.*)

REED. You'll do well to be less eloquent about doctors, Mr. O'Hara. You'll all do well to talk less about this epidemic. (BRINKERHOF *returns carrying an official document of some five or six pages.*) Epidemics are best not talked about. There's " Retreat." (*The three* SOLDIERS *salute and go.* REED *has turned to* BRINKERHOF.) Yes, Mr. Brinkerhof? (BRINKERHOF *proffers the document.*)

BRINKERHOF. From General Wood's headquarters. For you, sir.

REED. What is it?

BRINKERHOF. The army death list brought up to date, sir.

REED. (*Wincing as he takes document.*) Thank you, Mr. Brinkerhof. (*He turns and goes somberly up into laboratory, studying document as he goes. The sky is reddening with sunset.*

He is surprised to find AGRAMONTE *working at microscope.*
BRINKERHOF *goes.*) I didn't know you'd come in, Agramonte.
AGRAMONTE. (*Not looking up.*) Just now, doctor. To examine
this.
REED. Is it . . . is it from the dead boy you've just had down
there?
AGRAMONTE. (*As before.*) You didn't join me.
REED. (*Turning distressfully away.*) I was waiting for Carroll to
get back from Pinar. I didn't feel up to another autopsy today.
AGRAMONTE. (*As before.*) I can understand that.
REED. Still nothing?
AGRAMONTE. Did you expect anything? After two months of this?
And how many boys cut up? Did you still expect anything?
We've made a record for thoroughness at any rate, doctor.
REED. (*Shaken.*) I can't stand much more of this, Agramonte.
Have you looked over the army death list lately? They're our
boys!
AGRAMONTE. Yes, doctor.
REED. And I look out there over the sea and watch our trans-
ports steaming home and I daren't think what they may be carry-
ing! And we've taken Cuba on! Taken it on with this awful thing
smoldering in it! Smoldering and waiting for fresh fuel. For fresh
American fuel now, Agramonte! Waiting its chance to jump over
home to us! As it's been doing for over a hundred years! To
Philadelphia and New Orleans and . . . And to know we've had
it under our microscopes a thousand times and never seen it! And
men will die and go on dying for all . . .
AGRAMONTE. It is not an agreeable condition from my point of
view either, doctor. I am Cuban born.
REED. I didn't mean to offend you, Agramonte. It isn't easy to
admit one's failed. It shakes one's nerve. (*He sits smiling.*) I've
said to myself all this afternoon: " If Carroll brings me back
anything from Pinar, anything that even looks like a new
lead . . ." (CARROLL *has entered through the gathering dusk outside.*) Carroll!
CARROLL. Well, I did get here.
REED. What news from the camp at Pinar?
CARROLL. There's no doubt about your diagnosis. Pernicious malaria my eye! It's yellow jack and going great guns, too! Christ!
They're dropping like flies! (REED *turns away.*)
AGRAMONTE. Is that all you have to tell us?

19

CARROLL. I can't tell you a damned thing that we don't know already! There's nothing to do but wait and see how bad it gets.

AGRAMONTE. And I'm told General Wood's lost a third of his staff in the past month!

REED. At his mess they've been drinking toasts to the last to go. Now they've begun drinking to the next.

CARROLL. (*Nodding.*) And Wood knows it was yellow jack, not Rough Riders, that licked the Spaniards here. And it will lick us if we don't lick it first.

AGRAMONTE. There's no doubt about that.

REED. And our commission—you, Agramonte, and you, Carroll, and Lazear and I—we were sent down here to stop this horror! To isolate a microbe and find a cure! And we've failed! It isn't easy to admit that.

CARROLL. It's better than pretending you're getting somewhere.

REED. If I could only think of some fresh angle. . . .

CARROLL. We've tried every angle! Give it up, Chief! It's no use!

REED. I'm calling the Commission to disband it tonight. It won't be a long session. Then we'll go home.

CARROLL. Thank God! I hate wasting time! I've got to have something I can *see* and *get* at! Like that typhoid job before we came down here! Those flies traveled straight as an arrow from backhouse to mess hall! That was a job you could get some enjoyment out of! Let's go home and get on to something else! Only you'd keep me with you, wouldn't you, Chief? Hell, you know I'm a one-man dog. Christ! I know how you feel, though! (*An affectionate gesture from* REED *to* CARROLL.)

AGRAMONTE. The most we could do would be to keep on working. We have at least discredited everyone else.

REED. (*Desperate.*) And we're quitting. We're breaking the chain! Have we the right?

CARROLL. I can see I've stayed away from you too long.

REED. We know so little, Carroll. We know so little!

CARROLL. I ran into one puzzler out there at Pinar.

REED. I've heard enough puzzlers I can't solve.

CARROLL. This is a funny one. Case of a soldier. Sick July 12th. Died on the 18th.

REED. You reported him.

CARROLL. Didn't know he hadn't been near the disease for over a month before he took sick.

REED. (*Looking up.*) How was that?

CARROLL. They had him locked up in the guardhouse!

AGRAMONTE. Sure of that, Carroll?

CARROLL. And there he lay in that guardhouse for three days after, with eight other prisoners and they didn't catch it. Not even the one who slept in his blankets after he'd died. (" *Mess Call* " *sounds.*)

REED. (*Sharply.*) How about contaminated food or water?

CARROLL. The whole outfit ate and drank the same.

REED. The other eight may have been immunes.

CARROLL. Records don't show it. One came from Iowa, one from Maine, two from Wisconsin . . .

REED. The man may have been extra susceptible.

CARROLL. That might explain it. If *we* could explain why we don't catch it. (*But* REED, *caught in sudden thought, holds up his hand for silence.*) What?

REED. Nothing. I'll see you tonight. (AGRAMONTE *and* CARROLL *exchange a glance, but decide against asking questions.*)

CARROLL. After supper. All right.

AGRAMONTE. We'll go clean up.

REED. Eight-thirty, gentlemen. (AGRAMONTE *and* CARROLL *go out into the dusk, leaving* REED *alone. " Mess Call " sounds again, nearer and louder. The light concentrates upon the tensely thoughtful* REED, *until only his figure remains of the entire scene. A pause, then, solo.*) What was it crawled or jumped or flew through that guardhouse window, bit that one prisoner and went back where it came from? (*The scene goes into complete darkness. " Tattoo " sounds. Then the sky freezes to the green of tropic night and light shows* CARROLL, AGRAMONTE, GORGAS *and* TORY *talking easily on one of the flights of steps.* REED *stands apart on the edge of the shadow and* LAZEAR *lounges in the shadow above.* GORGAS, *aged forty-six, is friendly, keen and humorous.* LAZEAR, *thirty-four, is imaginative and wildly alive. Again the summer uniforms of officers of the Medical Corps.* TORY, *Colonel of the Marine Hospital Corps, is sixty, pompous and objectionable.*)

TORY. (*As the last notes of " Tattoo " die away.*) If you really have reached the end of your tether, Major Reed, my advice to you and to the members of your Commission is to call it a day. Go home. Give out a salty personal interview. Say your accomplishment here has been too technical for popular consumption. You will thus preserve the atmosphere of success which we all require for our reputations and to safeguard our service of our

21

glorious mistress, Science! You will then feel free to move on to pastures new, as the farmers say, and, as my friend, Major Gorgas, can assure you, you will be leaving this epidemic in worthy hands. The Marine Hospital Corps with which I have the honor to be connected . . . (LAZEAR *stirs irritably.* CARROLL *sits nodding approval.* REED *steps forward. But* GORGAS *interrupts.*)

GORGAS. Aren't you rather missing the point of this conference, Colonel Tory? It isn't General Wood's idea for anyone to go home. Wood wants us all working together on this. Wood's getting anxious for action. He watches me scrubbing and you fumigating and they tell him Reed's busy with microscopes. But he doesn't see any results. And it isn't only Cuba he's got on his mind. It's this whole Caribbean and Central American part of the world that we're getting involved in. It's Panama! How can we talk about a Panama Canal with yellow jack rampaging all over the place? This is the toughest problem Wood's governor-generalship has to grapple with and he's not going to let anyone quit. And neither am I, if I can help it! I'm the one Wood gets after and I'm tired of taking all the blame alone!

REED. I called the Commission to disband it tonight. Three hours ago I was certain we should disband. I hesitate now to propose continuing. The only course which remains open to us leads so far afield, seems so blocked with difficulty and beset with danger that I stand appalled before it.

GORGAS. You're being damn mysterious!

TORY. What is the course?

REED. To set our microscopes aside.

CARROLL. Say!

REED. And concentrate on new methods for prevention.

AGRAMONTE. How?

REED. By turning our minds to how yellow fever spreads, Agramonte. From man to man and village to village and even across the sea.

GORGAS. I should like to know something about that!

CARROLL. Not me. It's not my line. I'm a microscope man. I don't give a hoot in hell how it spreads. I'll work on cause or nothing.

TORY. I admire determination in men of science and if the Marine Hospital Corps hadn't covered the ground . . .

AGRAMONTE. Yes, doctor. What more can this commission add?

REED. (*To* AGRAMONTE.) I've come to suspect a middleman here. An infection carrier. In all likelihood an insect. Which we might hope to identify and which you, Gorgas, might subsequently wipe out.

AGRAMONTE. What kind of insect?

REED. Present evidence seems to point to a mosquito.

LAZEAR. (*Coming forward.*) Did you say mosquito?

GORGAS. (*A weary smile.*) You're not going off on that tangent, are you, Reed?

TORY. You can't be serious!

REED. I couldn't possibly be more so.

LAZEAR. And why not, Colonel Tory? If we find that a mosquito is the carrier of yellow fever and stop that, won't we have done our job? And what a job finding it's going to be! The kind that comes once in a lifetime! God bless you, Reed! Mosquitoes are meat and drink to me. (*General laughter except from* TORY.)

TORY. These fads are the curse of modern medicine!

LAZEAR. Fads? What fads?

TORY. Is medical science going insect mad?

LAZEAR. Where have you been at? Never hear of Smith's Texas fever tick? How about Bruce and the tsetse fly in Africa? Haven't Ross and Grassi just nailed malaria to a mosquito? I confirmed that myself! This fits in! This belongs! Insect mad! That's a hell of a thing to say these days, Colonel!

REED. Easy, Lazear.

TORY. Your junior colleague is a modern, Major. We have the dignity of science to consider!

LAZEAR. That girl! Holding a torch, standing in a niche!

TORY. We have enough theories about this already!

LAZEAR. There's still room for one that works!

TORY. We must draw some line against these radicals!

LAZEAR. Not so long since they called Pasteur a radical!

TORY. And so he was!

LAZEAR. May be! But he was right!

REED. (*Smiling.*) Easy, Lazear! I want to hear what Gorgas has to say.

GORGAS. (*Also smiling.*) Why the mosquito? Why not the flea, the louse or the homely bedbug?

LAZEAR. Let me answer that, Reed! (*To* GORGAS.) Because yellow jack's not confined to the louse and bedbug belt! The cleanest parts of town may be deadliest! You find fleas in the best families everywhere, but you don't find yellow jack outside mosquito districts! And it's worse in summer, which is mosquito season! You

23

see, I've got all the answers, Major Gorgas! If you want more, read Carter on the epidemic in Alabama! He came so near this!

GORGAS. You've silenced me, Lazear! You've silenced me!

TORY. (*Rising angrily.*) He has not silenced me! I fail to see why the Marine Hospital Corps with its long record in tropical epidemics should waste its time on inexperienced and untrained amateurs who . . .

GORGAS. This is no time for jealousies, Colonel Tory!

TORY. The Marine Hospital Corps, Major, does not stoop to . . .

LAZEAR. Aren't you the boys who diagnosed malaria at Pinar? Haven't you been fumigating Havana for three years? Who are you to talk!

REED. That isn't the subject in hand, Lazear!

LAZEAR. All right. One thing more and I'll shut up. We're not going home! We're not going to say: "Humanity and knowledge can both go hang, because we haven't got the guts to exceed instructions!" The hell with instructions! The hell with cause and cure! Reed's right and I'll go it alone if I have to! Only I won't have to work alone! There's a crazy old troglodyte here in this town! An old Scotchman with spectacles and side whiskers. Finlay, his name is. . . . (*Sensation.*)

TORY. (*Horrified.*) Finlay!

GORGAS. You don't mean old Finlay!

AGRAMONTE. Carlos Finlay?

LAZEAR. So you Cubans call him. . . .

TORY. You don't propose going to him for . . .

LAZEAR. Why not? He broke this mosquito idea years ago! He's got his particular guilty mosquito all picked out. I'm on my way to Dr. Finlay tomorrow morning and I'm going to say . . .

REED. I was just coming to Dr. Finlay, Lazear.

LAZEAR. We'll go see him together!

REED. I was just about to propose . . .

TORY. Do you *know* Finlay?

REED. I hope to know him before I'm many days older.

CARROLL. I never heard of him.

AGRAMONTE. I know him, of course. We Cubans revere and love him as a patriot. He did nobly throughout our revolution. As a scientist, however, I am afraid . . .

GORGAS. I know him, too. He was almost the first friend I made when I came here. He's a dear old fellow and a first rate physician. But he'll talk your ear off about that mosquito and if there'd been

24

anything in the idea, Reed, wouldn't nineteen years have brought it out?

TORY. Finlay's a crank. No more. A harmless crank.

REED. He may be, Colonel. He may be completely mad. If he is, though, he has a brave kind of madness. The jumping forward kind that's always too risky for the completely sane. You have your convictions. I have only my curiosity.

AGRAMONTE. I can think of nothing better to suggest.

CARROLL. This isn't my line. But go ahead anyway.

LAZEAR. (Through his teeth.) Finlay's got to be tried! There's no doubt about it!

TORY. (Slyly.) There is very grave doubt, if you'll allow me, doctor. The scheme isn't even possible.

LAZEAR. Why isn't it?

TORY. Could you draw any conclusion regarding mosquitoes without producing real cases of yellow fever from their bites?

LAZEAR. Did I say we could?

TORY. Aren't you forgetting that yellow fever's unlike other diseases? You can't give it to guinea pigs or monkeys or mice. You can't give it to any animal except man.

LAZEAR. I hadn't thought of that!

TORY. Think of it now and tell me how you could hope to test Dr. Finlay's mosquitoes by any conceivable experiment.

REED. (Quietly.) We haven't yet tried experimenting on men. (A general gasp. TORY rises astounded.)

CARROLL. For Christ's sake, Reed!

LAZEAR. By God! Get the mosquitoes! Feed 'em on sick men! Let 'em bite healthy men! See what happens!

TORY. (Stammering.) You don't propose using human guinea pigs!

REED. I hadn't thought of calling them by that name.

TORY. I can't believe my ears! Doctors, you call yourselves! Do you realize this is human vivisection! And might be manslaughter! Or even murder!

(More or less together.)

GORGAS. He's got you there, Reed!

CARROLL. You *are* going it pretty strong!

AGRAMONTE. Yes, I admit I hadn't thought of . . .

TORY. If Finlay were right and one of your victims died!

REED. If we fail at this, our victims, as you call them, will be none the worse for a few harmless mosquito bites. If we succeed, we shall have risked a few dozen lives to save countless thousands.

TORY. No! No! You've got to be stopped!

LAZEAR. We haven't started yet!

TORY. You're not going to start! Wait until General Wood hears of this!

REED. I'll take my chances, Colonel, with Leonard Wood, and if the members of this Commission . . .

AGRAMONTE. You can count on me, doctor!

CARROLL. We stand by, of course, Reed!

LAZEAR. This is an independent Commission, Colonel!

TORY. It isn't independent of Washington!

LAZEAR. Even Washington will think twice before it . . .

TORY. (*Shouting him down.*) American public opinion won't think twice! The American press and pulpit won't think twice! You know how they stand on animal vivisection! I'll go to them before I let you disgrace science and the army with this monstrous . . .

LAZEAR. Do you mean you'd run to yellow journals! Obstructing the very thing you pretend to . . . (MISS BLAKE *has entered below carrying a lantern.*)

MISS BLAKE. Dr. Agramonte?

AGRAMONTE. Yes, Miss Blake?

MISS BLAKE. Please overlook my interrupting. There's a case just come in and Dr. Ames very much wants Major Gorgas's opinion before they take him over to my ward. (*Two* ORDERLIES *enter carrying* MAJOR CARTWRIGHT, *sick unto death on a stretcher.* DR. AMES, *a vigorous Southerner in his forties, follows them in.* GORGAS *goes down to meet them. The others come down gradually.*) It's a Major Cartwright. I knew him in Matanzas before I came here. His papers show he had yellow fever two years ago.

AGRAMONTE. Dr. Ames is the physician in charge of our yellow fever ward, Major Gorgas. (GORGAS *nods to* AMES *and bends over stretcher.*)

AMES. If he hasn't got it now, what has he got?

GORGAS. (*To the sick man.*) Major Cartwright?

CARTWRIGHT. They're trying to tell me I've got yellow jack, Major! You can't have it twice!

GORGAS. (*Examining.*) Never heard of anyone's having it twice.

CARTWRIGHT. Well, I had it two years ago behind Santiago.

GORGAS. Yes, it was bad in Santiago two years ago.

CARTWRIGHT. I had a bad case, too. And just turning a little yellow doesn't mean . . .

26

GORGAS. It needn't mean a thing. (*He straightens up, nodding to* AGRAMONTE.)

CARTWRIGHT. That's why I didn't come over four days ago.

AGRAMONTE. It's a pity you didn't come four days ago. You might be more comfortable now. Your ward, Miss Blake. (MISS BLAKE *starts, then nods to the* ORDERLIES, *who carry* CARTWRIGHT *out.*)

CARTWRIGHT. (*As they go.*) I knew I couldn't have yellow jack! (*To* AMES, *who is following him.*) You ought to know better than to scare a man half to death! Nobody ever gets yellow jack twice! Lord, but I'm sick, though! (*He is gone, an attack of vomiting audible off-stage. The light has gone from the sky. As before, only the foreground group is lighted.*)

CARROLL. They've been calling yellow jack malaria at Pinar. Wonder what he had that they called yellow jack two years ago.

TORY. You don't mean he's got it?

GORGAS. (*Flatly.*) He'll be dead tomorrow. (REED'S *face sets.*)

TORY. And you'd have done that to men in cold blood! (*He can say no more, except:*) If you're ready, Major Gorgas, I'll bid these gentlemen a very good evening.

REED. (*Steadily.*) Good evening, Colonel. (*But the* COLONEL *is already on his way.*)

GORGAS. (*To* REED, *somewhat apologetic.*) Well, it turned out livelier than most medical meetings. Sorry I couldn't give you more support. It wouldn't have panned out, though. I'm right about Finlay.

REED. You may be.

GORGAS. That poor devil Cartwright certainly cut the discussion short! Just what was needed to drive the point home!

REED. Good night, Gorgas. (*Ad lib. good nights as " Call to Quarters" sounds.* GORGAS *goes, turns up into the laboratory,* LAZEAR *following, letting out the full hurt of his disappointment. The others in their turn follow into laboratory.*)

LAZEAR. Reed, if you had this in the back of your head why didn't you just tell us? Why did you have to let them in on it? We could have tackled it alone!

CARROLL. If you ask me, it's just as well!

LAZEAR. (*Hotly.*) I don't agree! We might have made history!

CARROLL. Yes. Or made damn fools of ourselves!

LAZEAR. Don't be so sure of that!

REED. (*Quietly.*) Did you think I'd be stopped by anything they

27

said? After that poor devil " drove the point home " ?

LAZEAR. Reed!

CARROLL. Now listen, Reed! You know what Tory can do to you!

REED. (*Strong because imperturbable.*) There's no doubt of what Colonel Tory can do; I see no reason, though, why he or anyone should know what we're up to from now on. (*Pause, then:*)

AGRAMONTE. (*Low.*) But, doctor, would it be possible to experiment on men in secret?

LAZEAR. (*Quick and low.*) It's got to be!

CARROLL. Men, though! (*Off-stage the* QUARTET *begins singing very softly.*)

QUARTET.

" Oh, the moonlight's fair tonight along the Wabash,
    From the fields there comes the breath of new-mown hay;
Through the sycamores the candle lights are gleaming,
    On the banks of the Wabash, far away."

CARROLL. Men, God Almighty!

LAZEAR. (*Quickly.*) That's got to be, too!

REED. (*Low but stern.*) I'm afraid so. I'm afraid so.

CARROLL. (*A whisper.*) Men . . .

(*The light dies on the laboratory as the screen closes. At the same time light shows two tents on either side of the stage. On the right* O'HARA *sits on his cot studying Gray's " Anatomy" while* BRINKERHOF, *seated on the cot opposite, undresses for his night's rest. On the left,* BUSCH *and* MC CLELLAND *sit on their cots drinking beer.* MC CLELLAND *is dozing.* BUSCH *also has a book.* O'HARA *looks up from his book.*)

O'HARA. Will you listen to this, now, John? (*He reads.*) " A thorough study of human physiology is in itself an education. Like the Atlantic between the Old and New Worlds, its waves wash the shores of the two worlds of matter and of mind. Through its waters, as yet unfurrowed by the keel of any Columbus, lies the road from one to the other." (BRINKERHOF *is impressed but baffled.*)

BUSCH. Get this, Mac. (*He reads.*) " You were horrified at our intending to do away with private property, but in our existing society private property is already done away with for nine-tenths of the population. In other words, you reproach us with intending to do away with your property. Precisely so; this is just what we intend." (*He looks up.*) Let 'em answer that! (*He sees that*

28

MC CLELLAND, *due to unconsciousness, is not interested. He resumes reading.* QUARTET *carries on with " Good-bye, Dolly Gray.")*

BRINKERHOF. *(To* O'HARA, *with the morbid fascination of a small boy.)* Let's see the picture of the unborn baby.

O'HARA. *(Learnedly.)* The embryo, it's called. *(He shows the picture.)*

BRINKERHOF. Do you mean to say I once looked like that?

O'HARA. It's hard for me to believe I ever did!

BRINKERHOF. *(A shudder.)* Guess I'll go brush my teeth. *(He finds his toothbrush and goes.* O'HARA *resumes reading.* MC CLEL-LAND *has roused himself.)*

MC CLELLAND. You read too much. It ain't good for a man to have so much on his mind.

BUSCH. *(Bitterly.)* Dough! You can't even be a good radical without dough! That's what gets me! If I had three hundred dollars . . . *(*O'HARA *closes his book disconsolately and sits staring before him in abject self-pity.)* I'd go back to my printing trade like I'm always saying. In my own shop like my old man had before me that the cops smashed up in Chicago when I was a kid. And I'd get out a paper that'd tell the workers the truth. I know a printing shop in Newark, New Jersey, I could buy in on if I had three hundred dollars. And the other partners all radicals like me.

MC CLELLAND. I wouldn't waste any three hundred on no workers. Not me! I'd buy me a little home back in Savannah and get me a wife and quit whoring around. I want to get back to Savannah and take my girl walking around the Plaza evenings.

BUSCH. *(Violently.)* And me! Do you think I don't want to get home to Chicago? And ride on the " El " and smell that old coal smoke again!

QUARTET. *(Carrying on from " Dolly Gray.")*

" Just tell them that you saw me,
        She said, they'll know the rest.
    Just tell them I was looking well, you know.
        Just whisper if you get a chance
    To mother dear, and say,
        I love her as I did long years ago."

(MC CLELLAND *and* BUSCH *are submerged in homesickness.* BRINKERHOF *has returned to* O'HARA.)

29

BRINKERHOF. You'll ruin your eyesight reading.

O'HARA. I wasn't reading.

BRINKERHOF. What were you doing?

O'HARA. Thinking that when God gives a man a call to a profession he should provide the wherewithal to answer. (*He proceeds morosely to undress.*)

BRINKERHOF. Now you mustn't get discouraged, John.

O'HARA. What is discouragement but submission to fate?

(BRINKERHOF *gets into bed.*)

MC CLELLAND. That's a beautiful song. I can't stand songs about mothers. I'm an orphan and I ain't thought of my mother in years and years.

BUSCH. I'm an orphan, too. But I'm a Jewish orphan.

MC CLELLAND. Drink some more beer.

BUSCH. (*As* MC CLELLAND *fills his glass.*) If that beer was rum I could drink it neat and never show it! That's how I am when I think about my ambitions.

MC CLELLAND. Me, too, when I get homesick. (*They drink up morosely.* QUARTET *carries on with* " Good-bye, my Bluebell!" O'HARA *has paused in his undressing, lost in melancholy and none too soon for the sake of decency.*)

O'HARA. To them that ask little what they ask may be given. You'll get the stripes and satisfaction of your sergeancy. And Mac will get his girl to marry and the satisfaction of her. And Busch may find the three hundred he's wanting to buy him his revolutionary printing press and spread death and destruction over all the land. For even that's little compared with the vision of service in my mind's eye, and the passionate conviction of my gifts for the same in my heart, and the need of a costly training before me and the wage of a private soldier in my pocket! (*He gets into his cot.*)

QUARTET. (*Softly, off-stage.*)

" When you hear dem bells go ding-a-ling . . .
        Boom. Boom. Boom. . . ."

BRINKERHOF. We all got to watch for our opportunities, John.

MC CLELLAND. We just got to wait for our chances, Chicago.

QUARTET. (*A little louder.*)

" All join round and a-sweetly you must sing,
        And when the . . ."

(*Light begins to grow slowly upon the laboratory.*)

BUSCH. When'll they come and where'll they come from, Mac?

BRINKERHOF. I'm a great believer in opportunities, John.

O'HARA. Thanks for the comfort and good night to you, John.

(*The light dims upon both pairs of* SOLDIERS *at the same time. Now the laboratory, its shelves, glassware and microscopes, shines with unearthly effulgence, as from within itself, and the four members of the* COMMISSION *still seated there seem prophetically to answer the soldiers' needs out of night and the future.*)

CARROLL. (*A whisper.*) Men, God Almighty! Men!

QUARTET. (*Crescendo to full volume.*)

" Verse am over and the chorus all join in,
There'll be a hot time in the old town tonight."

(*Darkness, then:*)

AGRAMONTE. I have the honor, Major Reed, to present my colleague, Dr. Finlay, for these many years a distinguished leader of our profession here in Havana. Dr. Finlay, this is Dr. Lazear and this, Dr. Carroll. (*Then bright sunlight and* DR. FINLAY *stands above, gravely and formally shaking hands with the four members of the* COMMISSION. FINLAY *is an elderly and bewhiskered little Scotchman. The ceremony of introduction completed,* FINLAY *leads his guests down to the foreground.*)

FINLAY. We shall sit here in the patio if you don't mind, gentlemen. My office is dark. I see your faces more clearly here in the sun. Make yourselves as comfortable as you can. (*They sit,* FINLAY *composing himself last.*)

REED. Shall we omit the preliminaries? Dr. Finlay can guess what our errand is.

FINLAY. (*With a wary smile.*) Men come to my house on many errands, Major. Bibliophiles to examine my Latin manuscripts. Revolutionists to discuss politics. My fellow scientists don't honor me so often.

REED. We come to join you, doctor, in the war you have waged these many years alone. We offer you our co-operation and ask your assistance.

FINLAY. (*On his guard.*) One thing at a time. We can discuss your co-operation later. What form of assistance had you expected of me?

REED. Your knowledge of your yellow fever mosquito.

31

AGRAMONTE.. And, specifically, doctor, the mosquito herself. As many specimens as you can spare.

FINLAY. Did you think I should have them flying about my house? Or in bird cages like canary birds?

AGRAMONTE. The eggs will do.

REED. You have the eggs, I think? (*But* FINLAY *draws back.*)

FINLAY. For nineteen years science has laughed at me, Major. At the cracked old Finlay and his mosquitoes. And nowhere more cruelly than through American army doctors. Now you come running to me to save your faces! I might enjoy laughing myself now. I have a sardonic sense of humor. Will you be surprised if I have no impulse to share my secret?

REED. We shall be deeply disappointed, Dr. Finlay.

AGRAMONTE. We shall hope to persuade you.

FINLAY. I wonder you have not come to me before.

AGRAMONTE. We were committed to a particular line of investigation.

FINLAY. At which you have failed.

AGRAMONTE. At which we certainly have not succeeded.

FINLAY. I could have told you you would be wasting time! The microbe of yellow fever is not to be found by any technique yet developed.

AGRAMONTE. The four of us have reached that conclusion.

FINLAY. The disease could have been conquered long since, however, had it not been for the stupidity of men of science . . . so-called!

CARROLL. Can't say that to us, doctor! We're likely to prove your case for you if you've got a . . .

FINLAY. (*Offended at once.*) Prove my case? You mean you doubt my discovery?

CARROLL. There isn't anything I don't doubt! Till I'm shown!

FINLAY. For thirty years I've battled with this disease and seen all other observable conditions change and only this one mosquito remain constant. The truth I gave out nineteen years ago, Dr. Carroll, was founded on observation . . .

CARROLL. That isn't proof.

FINLAY. Will any proof convince the fools who've doubted me?

CARROLL. Fools have to be convinced, Dr. Finlay. That's what they're for!

FINLAY. If this is your attitude, let me say forthwith that I have

32

no interest in your co-operation. (*The members of the* COMMIS-SION *are dismayed.*)

LAZEAR. This is what might be called unexpected!

AGRAMONTE. (*Breaking in.*) If you'll pause to consider, Dr. Finlay, that . . .

REED. (*Breaking in.*) Dr. Finlay can hardly include us among . . .

CARROLL. (*Breaking in.*) Get me right, Dr. Finlay! This isn't my line. But Reed . . . (*His manner becomes solemn.*) Walter Reed's a great man, doctor!

REED. Better leave that part to me, Carroll!

CARROLL. Well, God damn it, you are and I know what I'm talking about! (*Back to* FINLAY.) I ought to! It's his training made a scientist of me! Christ! I was a lousy lumberjack when he took me on! You're getting Walter Reed on this! And that's something you don't want to turn down!

FINLAY. (*Cold.*) I am not unmindful of Major Reed's reputation.

REED. I can't say as much for myself as Carroll's said, doctor. But I *am* a worker, a careful and thorough worker. And I shall go after this with all there is in me.

FINLAY. I have my own reputation to think of, Major!

CARROLL. (*Angry.*) Well, if you think that's going to suffer from . . .

FINLAY. (*Fairly shaking with indignation.*) I have cherished my great discovery for nineteen years! Do you expect me to give it up to you? To make use of it and get glory from it when I . . .

LAZEAR. (*Breaking in.*) Glory isn't the idea, Dr. Finlay!

AGRAMONTE. (*Breaking in.*) Not give it up, doctor! Share it!

FINLAY. (*Finally.*) No, gentlemen! No! I appreciate your disappointment, but . . . No.

CARROLL. Well, if he doesn't want to work with us . . .

LAZEAR. Go easy, Carroll. (*His own wild smile.*) Whether Dr. Finlay wants us or not we want him! To see his discovery through to a finish with us!

FINLAY. (*Somewhat cheered.*) You believe in my discovery, Dr. Lazear?

LAZEAR. (*Shining enthusiasm.*) Yes, I believe in it!

CARROLL. Now *you* go easy!

LAZEAR. (*Riding him down.*) It's simple! It fits into the scheme of things! It's got to be right!

FINLAY. It is!

LAZEAR. (*Ablaze.*) We know how many truths have to bide their

33

time and wait for the world to catch up with 'em! We know how many go down unrecognized! We're what you've been waiting for, Dr. Finlay! We're going to save your discovery for you and pull the whole tribe of science into line!

FINLAY. (*Enchanted.*) An admirable young man! And the look of the seeker in the eyes!

LAZEAR. All you need is one bang-up demonstration!

FINLAY. (*Drawing back.*) Doubt again! Proof again!

LAZEAR. Thank God for both of 'em and the stiffer we make 'em the better! Doubt and more doubt till there's no escaping proof! Then we'll set your discovery where it belongs! Where folks can see it! Up there! In the constellation of established fact!

FINLAY. You almost persuade me!

LAZEAR. Come along with us, doctor! You belong with us!

FINLAY. Why didn't you come nineteen years ago!

REED. I'm no stranger to waiting, Dr. Finlay. All my life long my prayer has been that I might in some way alleviate human suffering. I think this may be my chance as well as yours.

FINLAY. (*Desperate.*) What can you do more than I have done already?

CARROLL. No one man can do all of any job.

FINLAY. But the proof you demand lies beyond any man's power!

REED. We don't feel that!

FINLAY. (*Full blast.*) You show your ignorance, Major! Look at you! A gentle, kindly man! No better fitted for this than I was myself! This wants the courage to be ruthless! You cannot test my mosquito without risking life!

LAZEAR. We know that, but . . . (*But nineteen years of bitterness breaks out in* FINLAY.)

FINLAY. There is no " but " ! That is the bitter fact! Do you think I have not dreamed that dream myself! What if we do risk a few lives, I've said, to save countless generations for the future! How many times I've said it! It cannot be! Are you asking me to believe you will be allowed to experiment on your soldiers!

CARROLL. I don't like the idea myself!

REED. Since there's no other way. And since the need . . .

LAZEAR. What the hell! An army of occupation! Nothing to think about but rum and women! We've only to call for volunteers!

FINLAY. And then? What then?

AGRAMONTE. Why, then the demonstration!

FINLAY. (*Scornful.*) You live in your own little world of professionals. You forget that other world outside, where the humane and kind-hearted and Christian live and love their fellow men! They may send their sons off to be butchered in battle, but let one of you lift one finger in this war and they will engulf you! You will be destroyed! There will arise such power of public fury . . .

LAZEAR. (*In a whisper of suppressed excitement.*) All right, Dr. Finlay! Let the soldiers wait! They'll keep! They'll be there any time we need 'em! We'll start this off ourselves!

FINLAY. You, gentlemen!

REED. (*Kindling.*) The four of us!

LAZEAR. No. Only three. Agramonte's had yellow fever.

AGRAMONTE. (*Regretful.*) Yes.

CARROLL. Am I in on this?

LAZEAR. Don't you want to be?

CARROLL. I like to be considered before I . . .

LAZEAR. I'll try it first. You can follow me.

CARROLL. I can follow you, can I?

LAZEAR. (*Nodding.*) You've got five kids.

CARROLL. You've got a kid yourself.

LAZEAR. That's four less than you. We'll hold Reed back to see that we don't bungle and . . .

REED. Why didn't we think of this before?

LAZEAR. What a job it's turning out to be!

FINLAY. (*His vocal powers only just restored.*) But I can't have it, gentlemen! You must put this idea out of your minds at once!

LAZEAR. (*Laughing.*) Thought you wanted us to be ruthless!

FINLAY. But this is carrying things too far!

CARROLL. After all, there may not be any risk.

FINLAY. There is, doctor! Believe me, there is!

REED. Then the three of us should make easy marks!

CARROLL. If you're right!

LAZEAR. And your mosquitoes aren't too fastidious!

FINLAY. No! You are men of science! Your lives are valuable!

REED. Is any man's life worth more than the cause he risks it on? (*Pause, then:*)

FINLAY. (*Deeply stirred.*) You must let me thank you. Major Reed. My friends, all of you. You come to me after nineteen years. Strangers. You fill my life with hope as sudden music fills our

Cuban nights. I concede your skepticism and revere your courage. I am honored. Tell me how I may serve you.

AGRAMONTE. (*Suavely covering the embarrassment of the others.*) Let them have the eggs, doctor. I think you had better let them have the eggs.

FINLAY. When I give them into your hands I give you nineteen years of my life. Well, I do it gladly. (*He goes out. The four members of the* COMMISSION *eye each other in the most intense excitement, but each one in his own mood,* AGRAMONTE *worried,* CARROLL *amused,* REED *solemn,* LÁZEAR *white hot.* FINLÁY *returns carrying a porcelain dish covered with a gauze. He sets it down on the table to uncover it, the four members of the* COMMISSION *leaning eagerly forward. The light begins imperceptibly to fade until only the five faces are visible, the old Scotchman's lit with a religious fervor as he describes his great discovery.*) You have only to raise the water in that dish and those eggs will hatch the criminal. Beware of her. She isn't one of your wild marsh mosquitoes. She's your domestic pet. Shares your home with you, takes her siesta underneath your eaves, raises her family in your patio fountain and rewards your hospitality with death. How do I know? I know! I have a mystic's faith in this mosquito! You hold the key to yellow fever in your hands. I pray for your sake and all humanity's that you may turn the lock I failed to turn.

REED. Curious. Very curious.

CARROLL. They look like little black cigars.

LAZEAR. (*A dry whisper.*) Come on! Let's get going! (*Darkness. Then the* QUARTET *is singing again.*)

QUARTET. " After the din of the battle's roar,
　　　　Just at the close of day,
　　　　Wounded and bleeding upon the field,
　　　　Two dying soldiers lay.
　　　　One held a ringlet of thin gray hair,
　　　　One held a lock of brown,
　　　　Bidding each other a last farewell,
　　　　Just as the sun went down."

(AMES *is standing, below, between two cots in which* SOLDIERS *lie sick of yellow fever and* MISS BLAKE *looks on as he speaks over the singing.*)

AMES. I don't know any more about it than you do, boys. I'm

only a doctor. These lab experiments are 'way over my head. I get my orders to let 'em bring their mosquitoes in here to the ward to suck a few yellow fever germs out of your blood. You've got plenty to spare, so there's nothing for you to get excited about. My God, one little mosquito bite won't make you feel any worse than you do already. (AGRAMONTE *enters above and comes quickly down the stair. He carries a wire basket filled with test tubes, the mouths of which are covered with tightly stretched gauze.*) You back again so soon?

AGRAMONTE. Don't tell me I'm wearing out my welcome.

AMES. Oh, no! I was just preparing these new arrivals, that's all.

AGRAMONTE. (*Hesitant.*) I don't like to trouble them, but if you've explained . . .

AMES. Go ahead. They're too sick to mind. Skeeters hungry?

AGRAMONTE. They've been crying like babies. (*Then, to* MISS BLAKE.) If you'll turn back the blankets so I can get at him, Miss Blake . . .

MISS BLAKE. (*As she turns blankets back from first cot.*) Don't be afraid. Doctor isn't going to hurt you. (AGRAMONTE *selects a test tube from the basket and deftly inverts it, applying its mouth to the patient's abdomen. He taps the end lightly to jar the mosquito down towards the flesh.*)

AGRAMONTE. Tap. Tap. There! Don't move. They itch less afterwards if you let 'em finish.

AMES. (*Looking on.*) You're getting neat at that. Who taught you?

AGRAMONTE. Lazear.

AMES. Where did he learn?

AGRAMONTE. Malaria. (*Then, to the patient, as he removes test tube.*) There, that's all. That wasn't so bad, was it? Insect No. 47, Miss Blake.

MISS BLAKE. (*Noting it down on her pad.*) Insect 47. Infected from a severe case. Second day of illness. (*Then as she applies alcohol to the bite.*) Just a little medication to soothe the itching.

(AGRAMONTE *returns first test tube basket and selects a second.*)

AMES. Once you get your skeeters filled up with yellow jack blood, though . . .

AGRAMONTE. (*Wry.*) Yes, Ames?

AMES. What do you do with 'em back there in that lab of yours?

(*Pause, then:*)

AGRAMONTE. (*Evasive.*) Oh, various things. (*Then:*) Why?

AMES. I was wondering. There are some pretty brutal rumors going around.

AGRAMONTE. You mustn't believe everything you hear, Ames. (*Then, to* MISS BLAKE.) Next. (*Business as before.*)

MISS BLAKE. Don't be afraid. Doctor isn't going to hurt you.

AGRAMONTE. Tap. Tap.

QUARTET. "One thought of mother at home, alone,
    Feeble and old and gray,
One of the sweetheart he left in town,
    Happy and young and gay.
One kissed a ringlet of thin gray hair,
    One kissed a lock of brown,
Bidding farewell to the Stars and Stripes,
    Just as the sun went down."

(*Darkness, under cover of which the cots vanish. Then light again as* O'HARA, BUSCH *and* MC CLELLAND *enter above and come sauntering down the stairs.*)

O'HARA. (*Speaking over the music.*) Go on, Mac. Don't stop. I crave all information of a medical nature.

MC CLELLAND. He keeps the mosquitoes each one in a kind of a bottle and he starts at one end and goes straight through the place till every boy there's got a bite in the belly.

BUSCH. I wouldn't know what to make of a thing like that. I wouldn't believe it unless I seen it.

MC CLELLAND. I hope to tell you I ain't never seen it! And I hope to God I don't never see it! I got no wish to go inside that place!

O'HARA. Major Reed! There's a man for thinking up bright ideas!

BUSCH. I think it's a hell of an idea! It's just one more lousy trick they thought up to put over on us! My God, ain't sick boys got enough on their minds without scratching bites! They wouldn't stand for it only they ain't class conscious. (O'HARA *and* MC CLELLAND *lift their hands in protest.*) There can't be nothing in the idea at that! How could a little harmless bug like a mosquito carry a terrible disease like yellow jack?

O'HARA. The insect may be small, Chicago, but germs are smaller and it's a question of relative size and capacity.

BUSCH. You give me a pain with your medical information. Mosquitoes ain't insects. Insects is things that crawl and jump and bite.

MC CLELLAND. Lions do that and lions ain't insects. (" *Call to Quarters* " *sounds.*) There's " Quarters."

O'HARA. (*As they go.*) There's more here than meets the eye, Chicago. And only the few of us are privileged to grasp the mysteries of medical science. (*At the same time light grows on the laboratory and the screen, opening, shows* REED *seated at his desk facing the audience, deep in troubled thought.*)

REED. Brinkerhof! (BRINKERHOF *enters laboratory.*) Did you see the transport people?

BRINKERHOF. They're holding a stateroom for you, sir.

REED. What time does the transport sail?

BRINKERHOF. Six in the morning, sir. But you can go aboard tonight.

REED. Thank you.

BRINKERHOF. I'm sorry to hear you're thinking of leaving us, sir.

REED. It isn't my idea, Mr. Brinkerhof. I've been ordered home. (*Then:*) You haven't mentioned it to anyone?

BRINKERHOF. Not a soul, sir.

REED. Ask Major Gorgas to come in. Then see if you can locate Dr. Lazear and round up the other members of the Commission. (BRINKERHOF *salutes and goes.* REED *draws a long envelope from his pocket and extracts an official paper from it. He unfolds this, studies it and suddenly, with a gesture of desperate rage, begins pacing to and fro.* GORGAS *enters.*) Sit down, Gorgas! Well?

GORGAS. (*Pointing to paper.*) Are those the orders?

REED. To Washington by the first available transportation. (*And he throws paper angrily on desk.*)

GORGAS. Thought I'd find you all raging about it together.

REED. I haven't broken the news to the others yet. I waited for you.

GORGAS. (*Humorously distressed for him.*) Don't know what I can do for you, Reed. General Wood couldn't tell me any more than we know already. The orders came through, that's all. You'll find out when you get to Washington.

REED. I can't leave Cuba now! I can't let go of this job now! I'm too deep into it to get out now!

GORGAS. Your leaving needn't hold things up. Lazear and Carroll are both good men.

REED. I can't desert Lazear and Carroll now!

GORGAS. (*Curious.*) Sounds interesting.

REED. It's the confounded stupidity of it, Gorgas! And when you

39

begin fitting things together and see what's behind these orders!

GORGAS. Oh, Reed! Reed! We've been in the army too long for that! They've forgotten what they sent you here to do or they've found something else for you or they've just got tired of waiting . . .

REED. I know that's possible. (*Pause, then:*) But I think we owe this to your friend Tory!

GORGAS. (*Surprised.*) Tory? (*Then:*) Why Tory? (REED *decides on making a clean breast of things.*)

REED. You were out here with him that night a month ago. You heard him that night. He's been out here since. Seeing what he can see. Making inquiries. (*Then, with suppressed fury.*) Even asking questions of soldiers!

GORGAS. (*Incredulous.*) Have you started on that?

REED. With Lazear. So you see I've more than my own disappointment to think of.

GORGAS. (*Awed.*) Results?

REED. You never know when. (GORGAS *smiles, but* REED *continues with the deepest possible feeling.*) I've infected Lazear. I might be at sea and not know. And Carroll comes next. I might be in Washington with both of them down. I'd never forgive myself! Right now, Gorgas, this moment, Lazear's watching his temperature, waiting for the first sign . . . (*Then:*) I am deeply fond of Lazear. I know you don't believe in this, but you'll admit it's possible I'm right.

GORGAS. At any rate, I understand how you feel.

REED. Can't you do something to keep me here? (*A pause,* GORGAS *moving about. Then, with sudden decision:*)

GORGAS. Sure you want to stay?

REED. Gorgas!

GORGAS. No, I mean it! If Tory's responsible for these orders and you do want Lazear and Carroll to keep going, they may need your influence in Washington more than they need you here.

(REED *is impressed.*)

REED. If I do go and anything should happen?

GORGAS. I'll do what's expected of me. (*Then:*)

REED. I'll go. Thanks for giving me a reason.

GORGAS. If that's all I can give you . . .

REED. Won't you wish me luck?

GORGAS. At bringing Lazear and Carroll down with yellow fever? I'm afraid I can't go that far with you, Reed.

REED. Well, don't talk about it and . . . (LAZEAR *enters*.)

LAZEAR. How are you, Major Gorgas?

GORGAS. The important question is: how you are, Dr. Lazear.
(LAZEAR *turns surprised to* REED.)

REED. He had to be told.

LAZEAR. (*To* GORGAS.) I'm very well. (*He laughs*.) Seems a pity, doesn't it?

GORGAS. Does it? (*He gives up*.) The laboratory mind is beyond me! Good night, Reed.

REED. Good night, Gorgas. (GORGAS *goes*.)

LAZEAR. (*Quick and anxious*.) Was it wise to tell him?

REED. It couldn't be avoided.

LAZEAR. Why not?

REED. There were reasons.

LAZEAR. Has anything gone wrong? (*For answer* REED *grasps the younger man's shoulders with sudden intensity*.)

REED. You want to keep on with this, don't you, Lazear?

LAZEAR. (*Horrified*.) You're not thinking of stopping me yet?

REED. I'm thinking of you!

LAZEAR. (*Relieved*.) Is that all?

REED. That's all. (*Then his own feeling embarrasses him and he draws back*.) Still no sign?

LAZEAR. Normal as hell. (*He offers a clinical thermometer*.)

REED. (*Examining it*.) How long since?

LAZEAR. Just now. (REED *smiles, returning thermometer*.)

REED. Not even a headache?

LAZEAR. Without any temperature?

REED. That would be a good deal to ask! (*He backs off*.) No feeling here? (*His hands press his own groins*.)

LAZEAR. (*Repeating action*.) Don't think so.

REED. You'd know. All over your body. Let's look at Agramonte's record. (*He sits at his desk, pulling notebook towards him*. CARROLL *and* AGRAMONTE *enter, buttoning their tunics*.)

AGRAMONTE. You sent for us, doctor?

CARROLL. We were right in the midst of a card game. What's the idea?

REED. I'll tell you in a minute.

AGRAMONTE. Not Lazear! Lazear, it hasn't happened!

CARROLL. (*To* LAZEAR.) Don't tell us the skeeters have got you!

LAZEAR. No.

REED. (*To* LAZEAR.) How many days is it since . . .

LAZEAR. Since the last bite I took? Six.

REED. I should think you'd have shown something in six days.

(CARROLL *relaxes as usual.*)

CARROLL. Well, you can't keep on feeling fit indefinitely and not cast some shadow over this mosquito business.

LAZEAR. Did you expect things to be easy? They never are!

CARROLL. What do you say we give up mosquitoes and try seagulls!

LAZEAR. Go to hell!

CARROLL. I'd rather go home. I'm sick of this show.

REED. (*Deep in his notebooks.*) Sit down, Carroll. I'll come to you. (CARROLL *sits, well pleased with himself.*)

LAZEAR. (*Stubborn.*) If only our facts would keep up with our hunches what a cinch things would be! What if my first three bites haven't come off? What odds will you give me on my thirty-seventh? You can't let go once you're caught in a thing like this! There's always the chance of the lucky accident! There are plenty more combinations to try yet!

REED. (*Grim.*) Plenty.

LAZEAR. I can tell you one trick we've overlooked! (*He is walking about in his excitement.*) And it's the same Ross struck on with malaria. (REED *looks up.*) You can feed *those* mosquitoes *full* of malaria blood and they can't hurt a baby for two weeks afterwards! They've got to have a good two weeks to ripen! We haven't given our skeeters any time!

REED. (*To* AGRAMONTE.) How long has your oldest mosquito had to digest her meal of yellow fever blood?

AGRAMONTE. Twelve days. There are still three left from the first lot we infected. No. Two. One died yesterday.

REED. Both infected from good strong cases?

AGRAMONTE. One case five days along. The other six. Both cases fatal.

LAZEAR. They're the next combination! Come on, Agramonte! We'll try both!

REED. Both, by all means. (*To* AGRAMONTE.) Understand, Agramonte? (AGRAMONTE *nods.*) Lazear starts again with two ripe ones day after tomorrow. If they take. (*To* LAZEAR.) Use Carroll to confirm you.

CARROLL. They won't take. (LAZEAR *turns angrily, but* REED *cuts him off.*)

REED. (*To* CARROLL.) If Lazear still shows nothing by a week from Wednesday, Carroll, we'll start with you.

CARROLL. But, Chief, if Lazear still shows nothing in ten days, why do I have to . . .

REED. I'm giving orders.

CARROLL. All right, Chief. All right.

LAZEAR. (*Low.*) Call yourself a scientist!

CARROLL. What the hell!

REED. Can you keep this pair in order, Agramonte?

AGRAMONTE. The experiment itself should do that, doctor.

CARROLL. My heart may not be in this, but . . .

REED. You'll control your heart. If you were less pig-headed, Carroll, and you less hot-headed, Lazear, I should feel far more comfortable about . . .

LAZEAR. About what?

REED. I'll come to that. If either of you falls ill, let Gorgas know.

CARROLL. Gorgas! (REED *holds up his hand for silence.*)

REED. Ames is a good man, but I shall want Gorgas on hand, too. Your illness will mean the success of this, but you both mean a great deal to me.

CARROLL. Aren't you looking pretty far ahead, Chief?

REED. (*Riding him down.*) Whether this succeeds or fails, however, I demand unimpeachable workmanship, because nothing less will . . .

LAZEAR. Why are you going into all this, Reed?

REED. Do you think you can handle this alone?

AGRAMONTE. Alone?

REED. I'm putting it up to you. (*He hands* LAZEAR *the orders identified earlier by* GORGAS. LAZEAR *glances and stares blankly back.*)

LAZEAR. Called home!

CARROLL. Who?

AGRAMONTE. Not Reed!

LAZEAR. Yes. Reed.

CARROLL. (*Voiceless.*) My God! Let's see! (*He takes paper.*)

AGRAMONTE. (*Stammering.*) But you can't go, doctor! We can't get on without . . .

CARROLL. (*Pleading.*) Now, listen, Chief! You've got to stick with this! It isn't fair to . . .

43

LAZEAR. You certainly are putting it up to us! (*The light concentrates upon* REED *alone.*)

REED. We were four in this. Now you'll be only three. God bring you safely through, Carroll . . . and Lazear. (*Darkness. Then "Reveille" is sounded by the assembled field music. Then "Assembly" sounds. Then bright daylight shows the laboratory, its equipment augmented, now, by a considerable addition of glassware consisting of racks of the same gauze-covered test tubes which* AGRAMONTE *carried earlier to the yellow fever ward and of larger gauze-covered beakers.* CARROLL, *at his microscope, is deeply engrossed in the examination of a series of slides.* AGRAMONTE, *at the workbench, is entering infected mosquitoes in his record book. Behind the laboratory, back and forth against the sky,* LAZEAR *paces, restless and distraught. Sometimes he comes to the head of the stair on one side or the other.* SOLDIERS *are crossing the forestage,* O'HARA, BRINKERHOF, MC CLELLAND *and* BUSCH *included, buttoning their tunics as they go and grumbling.*)

MC CLELLAND. Drill and tote stretchers. Then stand inspection and drill some more.

BRINKERHOF. There ain't nothing for armies to do in times of peace *but* drill!

O'HARA. And the sweat oozing out of our armpits with the heat and the brains oozing out of our skulls with the monotony!

BUSCH. Militarism! Capitalism! Imperialism! (*They are gone.*)

COMMAND. (*Off-stage.*) Company, fall IN! (*Two or three late comers hurry across the stage.* AGRAMONTE *looks up.*) Company, attenSHUN! . . . Right DRESS! . . . FRONT! . . . Call the roll! (*The roll is called and answered diminuendo as the scene progresses.*)

AGRAMONTE. (*A smile, then, solo.*) Camp goes on and so do we, God help us! (*Then, solo, as he works.*) Insect Number Two Hundred and Fifty-three. Infected from a moderate case. Fifth day in hospital. (*He makes the entry.*)

CARROLL. They've got measles over in the enlisted men's barracks. I made 'em give me some bloods to play around with. You can't see a thing in measles bloods either, but they're a change from these damned mosquitoes.

COMMAND. (*Off-stage.*) Company, attenSHUN! . . . Squads RIGHT! . . . Forward MARCH! . . . (*Off-stage the sound of marching feet diminuendo as* LAZEAR *re-appears outside the laboratory.*)

LAZEAR. Ten days, Reed said! Ten days! Why in God's name did Reed have to go home and leave us? He'd know where we've gone wrong! He'd know! (*He goes.* CARROLL *has risen and gone to stand over* AGRAMONTE.)

AGRAMONTE. (*Solo as before.*) Insect Number Two-Fifty-four . . .

CARROLL. My God, will you never get enough of those?

AGRAMONTE. Could we get enough to satisfy Lazear? (CARROLL *laughs.*)

CARROLL. This epidemic petering out on him. Only had four new cases here since Sunday. That must be pretty disappointing to you boys.

AGRAMONTE. You look on matters too practically, Carroll. Are you blind to the artistry of science? (*A gesture takes in the laboratory.*) Each one in her own little glass house. Each one with her own ticket and number. It's nature in the raw reduced to method. Results or not, Carroll, look at it! (LAZEAR *is on the stairs.* CARROLL *points to him.*)

CARROLL. Look at him!

AGRAMONTE. He's disappointed.

CARROLL. He's bughouse.

AGRAMONTE. (*As before.*) Insect Number Two Fifty-five . . .

(LAZEAR *has turned suddenly into the laboratory, stripping off his coat. He snatches up a rack of test tubes, selects one and makes an annotation in a notebook.*)

LAZEAR. Number Ninety-eight. Infected from severe case on the day of death.

CARROLL. What? Again?

LAZEAR. Never say die, Carroll! Never say die! (*He is about to apply the mouth of the test tube to his arm.*)

AGRAMONTE. (*Stopping him.*) No, Lazear.

LAZEAR. Why not?

AGRAMONTE. You have had your turn. Even your second turn according to Reed's instructions, and . . .

LAZEAR. Even so . . .

AGRAMONTE. And the ten days since are passed without results.

LAZEAR. But we've got to keep on trying, Agramonte!

AGRAMONTE. Is there any good wasting any more time? (*A pause, then:*)

45

LAZEAR. (*Sober.*) No. (*And he returns the test tube to rack.*) None.

CARROLL. My God, have you boys really come to your senses?

(LAZEAR *turns angrily but* AGRAMONTE *cuts him off.*)

AGRAMONTE. Perhaps not according to your lights, Carroll!

CARROLL. No good wasting any more time, you said! I say: Pack up! Let the skeeters loose! Go home and . . .

AGRAMONTE. It was to be your turn after Lazear.

CARROLL. My turn!

AGRAMONTE. Those were Reed's orders.

LAZEAR. (*Steady.*) I'm stepping out. This is your show now.

CARROLL. Thanks.

LAZEAR. I hope you mean that. Because there's nothing wrong here except with me.

CARROLL. I can see there's plenty wrong with you.

LAZEAR. You needn't sneer. I may be a natural immune. Some men are. You'll give us the real test. If it fails with you, I'll begin to worry. Not before.

CARROLL. Ever hear the word " monomaniac " ?

LAZEAR. (*Smiling.*) It fits me like a glove. (*He offers* CARROLL *the test tube just now rejected.*) Here's Number Ninety-eight waiting for you. Are you ready?

CARROLL. Don't point that thing at me!

AGRAMONTE. Forgive me, Lazear, for interfering again, but in my opinion he is not quite ready.

LAZEAR. Why isn't he? I was!

AGRAMONTE. I should like to see more precise preparation than we have made thus far. I should like to see . . .

CARROLL. I won't be rushed into this!

LAZEAR. Who's rushing you?

AGRAMONTE. You are, Lazear! He's right . . .

LAZEAR. (*Wild again.*) Either you go through or you don't! But if you're going, for God's sake, go! And pray for the lucky accident! That's all science amounts to, anyway!

AGRAMONTE. Not quite, Lazear! If you will permit me to say one word . . .

LAZEAR. What is there to say? He promised Reed!

CARROLL. I don't care if I did! Reed knows I've got no damned use for this! Grown men coaxing a bottled mosquito to bite 'em!

Sucking thermometers for days afterwards, my God! Can't you see that's funny?

LAZEAR. What's funny about it?

CARROLL. You are! You're a scream! Sunk one minute and crazy wild the next! I can't keep up with you! I can't be bothered with you! I happen to be gifted with horse sense!

LAZEAR. Well, if that isn't a liability!

AGRAMONTE.. Please!

CARROLL. Call yourself a scientist!

LAZEAR. Hell, I don't care whether you go through or not!

AGRAMONTE. Much better not go through unless you can do it properly.

LAZEAR. If you're trying to help him welch on this . . .

AGRAMONTE. I have not said that.

CARROLL. Who says I'm welching? I'm going through. But only to humor you, Lazear! (*Quick with hope,* LAZEAR *again offers test tube.*)

AGRAMONTE. I have tried to say that if we cannot do this properly we had much better not do it at all.

LAZEAR. For God's sake, quit butting in! (*He shoves entire rack of test tubes towards* CARROLL.)

CARROLL. I don't want any of those!

LAZEAR. These happen to be from the deadliest cases, Carroll.

CARROLL. (*Grinning.*) I don't like their expressions. (*An exclamation of disgust from* AGRAMONTE.)

LAZEAR. I believe you're scared.

CARROLL. I wouldn't feel so damn foolish if I were! (*He finds a single tube in a basket set apart.*) What's this one all alone by herself?

LAZEAR. (*Looking.*) Number Forty-six. (*Then, to* AGRAMONTE.) It's the one we fed on that boy two weeks ago. The boy they'd just brought into the ward that day.

AGRAMONTE. That case hadn't even begun to develop, Carroll.

CARROLL. (*Grinning.*) Are you letting the poor thing starve because she . . .

AGRAMONTE. I had set her aside to infect her properly!

LAZEAR. Why do you have to waste time on that measly thing! I took mine from fatal cases! Why can't you?

CARROLL. A mosquito's a mosquito!

LAZEAR. Why can't you stick to routine?

CARROLL. Will you, for Christ's sake, let me have my fun with

47

this God-damn nonsense? (*He has stripped off his coat and is rolling up his sleeve.*)

AGRAMONTE. I warn you, you are being both slovenly and frivolous about this!

CARROLL. (*Grinning delightedly back.*) Come on, Black Beauty!

(AGRAMONTE *turns angrily out of the laboratory. But* LAZEAR *watches fascinated as* CARROLL *applies the mouth of the test tube to his forearm.*) Bite me!

COMMAND. (*Through the darkness.*) Port ARMS! . . . Order ARMS! . . . Right shoulder ARMS! . . . Port ARMS! . . . Order ARMS! . . . Parade REST! (*Then, as light shows the laboratory again.*)

AGRAMONTE. (*Angry.*) I have come to the end of my patience, now! (*And the three are discovered as before except that they now wear their laboratory work coats and that* AGRAMONTE *now dominates the scene.*) I have worked for you as your clerk! I have kept your records! Now I shall tell you both what I think of you! And I ask you: Is this a scientific experiment or . . .

LAZEAR. (*Hotly.*) You're damn right it is!

AGRAMONTE. It does not have that appearance for me! (*He swings on* CARROLL.) You! Are you not supposed to be testing infection by mosquito? Yet you went to the autopsy room this morning! You performed an autopsy on a man just dead of yellow fever! When you are testing one source of infection you deliberately expose yourself to another! If you *were* to become infected by the mosquito, how would you know, I ask you, how would you know which source of infection to hold responsible?

CARROLL. (*His temper also lost.*) Do you expect me to chuck my real work to test an idea he's already exploded?

AGRAMONTE. (*Topping him.*) I protest for more than this one idea! I protest for all scientific workmanship! Unimpeachable workmanship Reed demanded of you! And from the very day you offered to prove Dr. Finlay's case, I have warned you against rushing into things without preparation! Without thought or precaution!

CARROLL. Will you, for God's sake, quit yapping at me!

AGRAMONTE. I yap at Lazear, too!

LAZEAR. What can I do? Look what I'm up against! Has he even watched his temperature these last four days?

CARROLL. Go to it, boys! Then maybe I'll get some peace!

AGRAMONTE. When you were letting mosquitoes bite you in dozens! Were you not then exposing yourself in a hundred ways? If you had become infected then, could you have proven any more than Carroll?

LAZEAR. I'd have been so happy I wouldn't have cared!

AGRAMONTE. Is that workmanship?

LAZEAR. I'd have known what gave it to me!

AGRAMONTE. Is that science?

LAZEAR. It's the way I am!

CARROLL. Why in hell are you making this row now? If either one of us had come down you might have some kick. But we haven't come down and all this adds up to is theology!

AGRAMONTE. (*Quiet but stern.*) A time comes, Carroll, when a man must turn and speak out for his standards. I have made workmanship my religion. You will laugh and tell me I have a Latin mind. I have made my protest.

LAZEAR. (*Resolved but sober.*) No hard feelings. You're right. Workmanship now. Discipline. (*He turns to* CARROLL.) We're in earnest now. We won't count your playful attempt the other day. We'll pick out your next ourselves. No more rushing things, though. This time you go into isolation before we let any mosquito touch you.

CARROLL. Do I!

LAZEAR. Where nothing gets at you for a good two weeks.

CARROLL. All by myself?

LAZEAR. Then if you come down we'll know why.

CARROLL. I'll be God-damned if you put any more over on me! I'm through! I'm putting what I just got out of that dead spiggoty under the microscope for one last look. Then I hop a boat for home and kiss yellow jack good-bye!

LAZEAR. (*To* AGRAMONTE.) Now do you see what I'm up against?

(AGRAMONTE *clutches his head in despair.*)

CARROLL. (*Fortissimo.*) Coop me up for two weeks!

LAZEAR. (*Topping him.*) All right, you bloody, pig-headed clown! You can explain to Reed, though!

CARROLL. Sure I can! Think Reed would expect me to let you put this one over! Think Reed doesn't know me better than that! Coop me up? I couldn't stand it! I'm an active man. I've got to use my mind! This damn thing's got me crazy as it is! It's got me all off my feed! That's a fact! It has! (AGRAMONTE *pricks up his*

49

ears. CARROLL *sits again, pleading with* LAZEAR.) I'm sorry, Lazear. But you can't keep on day after day getting nowhere at something you've got no use for and not feel the effects! It wears you out! It gets you all run down! I woke up this morning feeling . . .

AGRAMONTE. (*Low but sharp.*) How?

CARROLL. Like hell. And I made up my mind then . . .

AGRAMONTE. (*Rising and circling him for a closer look.*) How like hell?

CARROLL. How would a man of my type feel after a month of this?

AGRAMONTE. Headache?

CARROLL. Head's felt like a dog's breakfast all morning! Shouldn't wonder if I've picked up some malaria. Once you get run down, you know, anything . . .

AGRAMONTE. Have you examined your blood for malaria?

CARROLL. (*Indicating microscope.*) Just now. Didn't find anything but . . .

AGRAMONTE. Feverish?

CARROLL. Not particularly. No.

AGRAMONTE. (*Very distinct.*) Blood negative and no fever. Somehow I doubt its being malaria, Carroll. (LAZEAR *looks up, a wild light in his eye.*)

LAZEAR. Carroll, you lousy bum!

CARROLL. What?

LAZEAR. You've got yellow jack!

AGRAMONTE. Yes, I was going to say . . .

CARROLL. (*Incredulous indignation.*) I have not got . . .

LAZEAR. He's got it, Agramonte! I know he's got it!

CARROLL. (*To* AGRAMONTE.) Will you listen to this maniac wishing yellow jack on me!

LAZEAR. You ought to be wishing it on yourself! What have we all been sweating over here! Isn't it four days since you took your bite? Four days may be schedule! We don't know that it isn't!

AGRAMONTE. From *that* mosquito?

LAZEAR. She may have had something in her after all! We don't know! We don't know! (*He shouts.*) Brinkerhof!

AGRAMONTE. What do you want with . . .

LAZEAR. I want Ames here!

CARROLL. You'll turn into a mosquito yourself if you don't watch out! (BRINKETHOF *enters.*)

LAZEAR. (*To* BRINKERHOF.) Fetch Dr. Ames.

CARROLL. Do nothing of the sort!

50

LAZEAR. Go on! (BRINKERHOF *runs out.*)

CARROLL. I'm damned if I see Ames! When I want a doctor . . . What in hell are you laughing at?

LAZEAR. (*Splitting with laughter.*) Only humoring me! Went into the autopsy room and exposed yourself this morning! Won't it be the God-damnedest joke on you if you have got yellow jack and die of it!

CARROLL. Joke!

LAZEAR. Yes, joke! (*To* AGRAMONTE.) Look at him! He's getting scared I'm right!

CARROLL. (*Frightened in spite of himself.*) You're a son of a bitch, Lazear!

LAZEAR. (*Choking.*) The laugh's on you, Carroll, you bungling . . . (*But* AGRAMONTE *turns to shake* LAZEAR.)

AGRAMONTE. Stop it, Lazear! That's too horrible! (LAZEAR *is sobered as* AMES *enters.*) Here's Ames now.

AMES. Did you want me for something?

CARROLL. No. Lazear did. The damn fool's trying to tell me I've got . . . (*On his feet, however, he totters and* AGRAMONTE *catches his elbow.*) Take your hands off me! (*But his own hand goes to his dizzy brow.*) Come over to my quarters, Ames. There's nothing wrong with me. All I need is a little quinine and a headache powder and I'll be . . . (*He is gone,* AMES *following bewildered.*)

LAZEAR. Agramonte!

AGRAMONTE. What?

LAZEAR. I'm scared to death.

AGRAMONTE. What of? That Carroll's got yellow jack or that he hasn't?

LAZEAR. Both.

(*Darkness. " Drill—First Call " again. Then again light on the laboratory and* LAZEAR *sits in his shirtsleeves at the microscope. while* AGRAMONTE, *now in uniform, paces to and fro evidently under a severe strain.* FINLAY *enters to them in a tremolo of mingled delight and awe.*)

FINLAY. I have seen Dr. Carroll! Whatever doubts you may have had yesterday, there can be no question now! First I was sorry for him! Then I remembered to thank God!

LAZEAR. (*Looking up in excitement from microscope.*) There's not a trace of malaria in the blood! Malaria would have shown

51

CARL A. RUDISILL
LIBRARY

itself by this! (*He is on his feet.*) Let's celebrate, Dr. Finlay! Let's get drunk!

AGRAMONTE. (*Full force at both of them.*) What you and Dr. Finlay may or may not believe is not evidence, and you cannot deceive yourselves that it is! (*The pair fairly scream back at him.*)

FINLAY. A man has been bitten by my mosquito!

LAZEAR. And has got yellow jack as a result!

AGRAMONTE. Not necessarily as a result!

FINLAY. What he did, where he went yesterday, is of no importance!

ARGAMONTE. It is of the most disastrous importance!

LAZEAR. He came through three months of exposure before he was bitten!

AGRAMONTE. That is not proof!

FINLAY. It was my mosquito that infected him!

AGRAMONTE. We don't know that!

LAZEAR. You're splitting hairs!

AGRAMONTE. I'm talking science! You know that we have bungled Carroll's sickness! You know his life will be wasted if he dies!

LAZEAR. There's no good looking on the dark side, is there?

AGRAMONTE. You know that is what you must report to Reed!

LAZEAR. Reed will know that we've got this! Here! Under our fingers!

AGRAMONTE. Where?

LAZEAR. We *have* got it! This *must* be the mosquito!

AGRAMONTE. You *want* to believe that!

LAZEAR. I've *got* to believe it! Carroll may die!

AGRAMONTE. All right! Tell me why that one mosquito should succeed with Carroll when fifty failed with you and I will believe! But I must know why, Lazear, before I can! (*Pause, then:*)

LAZEAR. (*Defeated.*) Damn your bloody logic, Agramonte!

FINLAY. Yes. When you know that you will know everything.

LAZEAR. Yes. *When.*

FINLAY. Oh, I realize it may be difficult to determine. You must produce another case! That *will* be proof and confirm Dr. Carroll! So that his life need not be wasted if he dies. So that my mosquito may come into her own!

LAZEAR. How?

FINLAY. I leave that to you.

LAZEAR. Thanks. (*A pause, then desperately he turns to the shelves.*) Which one was Carroll's?

AGRAMONTE. (*Very steady.*) Dated the twenty-seventh.

LAZEAR. (*Reading off the labels.*) The twelfth. Mine. No good. Fourteenth. Sixteenth. Eighteenth. Mine. All mine. (*He finds it.*) Here. Carroll. The twenty-seventh. (*He picks tube out of rack.*) Read me the record.

AGRAMONTE. (*Glancing down upon the page of an open note-book.*) " Insect infected from case in second day of disease. Symptoms not definite but subsequently well developed." (LAZEAR *holds up his hand for silence.*)

LAZEAR. (*Strangely absorbed.*) Second day! How many others did we feed on patients that early in the disease?

AGRAMONTE. I don't know. A few.

LAZEAR. You've got 'em in the record, haven't you?

AGRAMONTE. Certainly. (*He runs his finger down page.*) Here's another from a case in the second day. Here's a third day. Here's a first.

LAZEAR. And I was too smart to try any of those!

AGRAMONTE. You didn't want to waste time on them.

LAZEAR. Waste time! (*Then:*) Christ! Oh, Christ!

AGRAMONTE. What is it?

FINLAY. Dr. Lazear! (*He rises.*)

LAZEAR. (*Very deliberate.*) Suppose—mind, I'm only thinking aloud—but here's this microbe no one has ever seen. Suppose it's in the blood only the first few days. Before you really know what's wrong with you . . .

FINLAY. What could become of it afterwards?

LAZEAR. I don't know!

AGRAMONTE. (*Low.*) Do you mean that it might go somewhere else? Out of the blood?

FINLAY. (*Low.*) Or change? Or die after the first few days?

LAZEAR. (*His throat painfully dry.*) I don't know. I don't know. If there were anything in the idea, though, we've been wasting time feeding our skeeters on advanced cases. There wouldn't have been any microbes left in them. And that would explain why I couldn't . . .

AGRAMONTE. (*An awed whisper.*) And Carroll could!

FINLAY. (*An awed whisper.*) Have you found it at last? (*But* LAZEAR *can only smile weakly.*)

LAZEAR. It's too easy. Things can't be that simple.

FINLAY. Truth can.

AGRAMONTE. I wish that Reed were here.

LAZEAR. Yes. So do I. (*Dazed, he holds out test tube to* AGRA-MONTE.) Put all your early birds in a special rack. (*He turns to* FINLAY, *as* AGRAMONTE *proceeds to obey*.) If this is the trick, I never ran any risk at all. And I may be as susceptible as any man. And I could be the case to confirm Carroll.

AGRAMONTE. (*Firmly*.) Only you'd have to be isolated for two weeks first.

FINLAY. And in two weeks Dr. Carroll will be well or dead.

LAZEAR. (*Wild again*.) We can't leave him lying there if he's done this! We can't let him die without knowing what he's done! God, why can't we come out in the open now and commandeer a whole regiment to experiment on? ("*Recall*" *sounds*.)

FINLAY. You'll come to it! I told you in the beginning!

COMMAND. (*Off-stage*.) Company, disMISSED!

LAZEAR. (*Insane*.) God send me one pure, unsuspecting human guinea pig! One I can't bungle! One I can cram down the whole world's throat! All wool! A yard wide! Fireproof! Watertight!

(SOLDIERS *cross stage, returning to their barracks from drill,* O'HARA, BRINKERHOF, BUSCH *and* MC CLELLAND *among them. They mop their brows and their guns are slung idly, any way, for comfort. Some of them are singing as they cross.*)

SOLDIERS. "Well, I guess I'll have to telegraph my baby,
I needs some money bad, indeed I do!
My Lucy is a very generous lady,
And I can always touch her for a few.
I find the Western Union a convenience,
No matter where I roam,
So I'll telegraph my baby,
She'll send ten or twenty maybe,
And I won't have to walk back home."

(FINLAY *is leaning out of the laboratory.*)

FINLAY. Dr. Lazear!

LAZEAR. What?

FINLAY. Have you never heard of a prayer being answered?

LAZEAR. No, doctor. Those are our Medical Corps boys. They know too much.

FINLAY. All of them? All? Can't you find one?

(*The* SOLDIERS *have cleared away, leaving one—*PRIVATE DEAN, *a nondescript, hick American—looking up at laboratory.*)

LAZEAR. Do you know that cavalryman out there, Agramonte?

AGRAMONTE. No, I don't think so. (*Then he understands.*) No, Lazear! Not that! (LAZEAR *is on his way out of laboratory.*)

LAZEAR. Why not?

AGRAMONTE. (*Stopping him.*) Will your conscience let you?

LAZEAR. What's conscience got to do with it? (*He has broken away and runs down steps to* DEAN.)

AGRAMONTE. (*To* FINLAY.) Stop him, Dr. Finlay!

FINLAY. And let Dr. Carroll die without confirmation? (*He follows* LAZEAR *down. Off-stage the* QUARTET *strikes into " Goodbye, Dolly Gray."*)

LAZEAR. (*To* DEAN.) Good morning.

DEAN. (*Saluting lamely.*) Good morning, sir.

LAZEAR. I don't think I've seen your face before.

DEAN. I'm what might be called a stranger over this way, sir.

LAZEAR. Were you looking for someone?

DEAN. No, sir. Just looking around.

LAZEAR. (*A deep breath and a glance at* FINLAY, *then:*) Would you like to come in?

DEAN. In where, sir?

LAZEAR. Into the laboratory.

AGRAMONTE. (*Low.*) No!

FINLAY. Come in, young man! Come in! (*He bows* DEAN *up the stair.*)

DEAN. I wouldn't mind. This the place where you got all the mosquitoes? (*He looks about. Turning to* LAZEAR.) I've been hearing quite a lot about your mosquitoes, sir.

LAZEAR. Oh? What have you heard?

DEAN. Well, you know how the boys talk.

FINLAY. What do they say? Tell us. We don't mind.

DEAN. They say you're raising 'em for pets.

LAZEAR. That's not far wrong.

DEAN. You sure got plenty of 'em. I seen a flea circus once. Can these do tricks?

FINLAY. We have one here who has just learned a fine trick.

LAZEAR. That is, we hope she has!

DEAN. She? A lady, is it?

LAZEAR. We don't bother with anything else.

FINLAY. Except when one of them needs a husband.

LAZEAR. We keep the husbands all together in that jar there.

DEAN. (*Examining.*) In that jar? Are those the husbands?

55

FINLAY. For breeding purposes.

DEAN. Oh, yes, I know about breeding! I was raised on a farm. Do mosquitoes . . . ? (*He seeks for the word, but cannot find it.*) Do they?

LAZEAR. Oh, yes.

DEAN. I'm interested in natural history. (*He turns to examine others.*)

LAZEAR. Where have you been keeping yourself the last few weeks?

DEAN. The last two weeks I been in hospital here. Before that I was stationed at . . .

LAZEAR. (*To* FINLAY.) Two weeks in hospital!

FINLAY. (*To* DEAN.) What was the trouble?

DEAN. Well, I . . . The fact is . . . Kind of got poisoned . . . (*Embarrassment.*)

FINLAY. Young men haven't changed. (*To* LAZEAR.) I don't think that presents any obstacle? After all, two weeks in hospital . . .

LAZEAR. You haven't been near the contagious wards, I hope?

DEAN. Oh, nothing like that! All I had was a . . .

LAZEAR. Haven't been near anyone sick with yellow fever?

DEAN. Jesus, I hope not! I mean I hope not, sir.

FINLAY. How much longer are they keeping you in hospital?

DEAN. They just let me out. Just now.

LAZEAR. Oh! Where will you go?

DEAN. My outfit's sailing home in a week.

LAZEAR. (*A prick of conscience.*) Home!

DEAN. Got to be done some day.

FINLAY. You're not pleased to be going home?

DEAN. You don't know my home, sir.

FINLAY. No.

DEAN. It ain't worth while. I wish they'd kept me here a few days longer. Enough for the outfit to get off without me.

LAZEAR. What's your name?

DEAN. Dean. William H. Troop A. Seventh Cavalry.

FINLAY. Married, Mr. Dean?

DEAN. I was going to be but I give it up.

LAZEAR. That doesn't count.

DEAN. (*Agreeing.*) That ain't worth while either.

FINLAY. Well, now, that all depends on how you look at it, Mr. Dean. (*General laughter and so disarming that* LAZEAR *seems not to notice what he is doing when he picks up the fateful test tube.*)

56

LAZEAR. How would you like to give Black Beauty her lunch?

DEAN. Black Beauty?

FINLAY. That trick mosquito I told you about.

DEAN. You mean for her to bite me?

LAZEAR. That's all. Roll up your sleeve.

DEAN. (*Drawing back.*) No. No, I don't think I'd care to do that, doctor. Just something about it don't strike me.

FINLAY. You're bitten by mosquitoes every day!

DEAN. That ain't the same as giving 'em lunch off you!

LAZEAR. Come on, now, Mr. Dean! Roll up your sleeve!

DEAN. (*Beginning very unwillingly to comply.*) It ain't natural, doctor!

FINLAY. Young man, he's offering you a great honor!

DEAN. I don't get this! (LAZEAR *applies mouth of tube to* DEAN's *forearm, tapping the end precisely as* AGRAMONTE *did previously but with even more deftness.*)

LAZEAR. (*To* DEAN.) Don't move!

DEAN. Makes me feel kind of funny!

FINLAY. (*Closing in on him.*) Look the other way, Mr. Dean.

LAZEAR. We've got a few more here that are hungry, too. You wouldn't mind giving them a meal while you're at it?

FINLAY. Certainly not!

LAZEAR. Then, Agramonte, if you'll just push that special basket over here where I can reach it? (AGRAMONTE *obeys mechanically.*)

FINLAY. We may have something of real interest to tell Dr. Carroll in a few days' time. (LAZEAR *has removed test tube. But he does not relinquish his grip on* DEAN's *wrist.*)

LAZEAR. That's the idea, doctor. (*He selects another test tube.*) Now, Mr. Dean . . . (*Darkness.*)

MISS BLAKE. (*Through the darkness.*) Quiet now, Dr. Carroll. Save your strength. You'll feel much more comfortable if you just relax. (*The bleak light of early morning slowly reveals* CARROLL *sick unto death on a hospital cot attended by* AMES *and* MISS BLAKE. LAZEAR *sits morosely apart.* AMES *is listening to the sick man's heart with his stethoscope. The scene is played below, the laboratory screen being closed.*)

CARROLL. (*Feeble, but in the best of good humor.*) If you can keep that heart of mine going, Ames, you're a better man than I think.

(LAZEAR *turns wretchedly.*)

AMES. I can't even hear your heart till you quit talking!

CARROLL. Helps me to talk. Keeps me from going out.

AMES. Go out if you want to. Won't hurt you any.

CARROLL. Going out's not so bad. Coming back's getting harder.

(AMES *folds stethoscope and goes to* MISS BLAKE.)

AMES. What time did you give that last injection?

LAZEAR. I gave it at three this morning.

AMES. (*To* MISS BLAKE.) Get another ready. (LAZEAR *rises*.) She'll do it. (LAZEAR *sits again heavily.* MISS BLAKE *goes out.* AMES *turns to* CARROLL. *Then:*) He's out again. Think you can keep your eyes open a few minutes longer?

LAZEAR. (*Rising.*) What do you want me to do?

AMES. Just sit here. It's seven-thirty. I ought to go look over the morning sick list.

LAZEAR. Go ahead. (AMES *is going, but* LAZEAR *stops him.*) If you find any new customers in the yellow jack ward, I'd like to know. (AMES *eyes him curiously, then:*)

AMES. I don't expect I will find any.

LAZEAR. You might. (*But* AMES *is gone. Then* LAZEAR *goes groggily to look down on* CARROLL. *Then, solo.*) For God's sake, get a move on, Private Dean! (*Then:*)

CARROLL. That you, Lazear?

LAZEAR. You back with us again?

CARROLL. I come and go. It's very interesting. Ames and that damn nurse gone? I hate nurses.

LAZEAR. Ames doesn't want you talking.

CARROLL. The hell with Ames. I want you to know the irony of this isn't wasted on me.

LAZEAR. Think it's wasted on me?

CARROLL. Took me quite a while to get around to it. I've got to die to appreciate it completely.

LAZEAR. You don't have to die if you fight.

CARROLL. You said it would be a joke on me. That was your idea.

LAZEAR. For God's sake, Carroll!

CARROLL. I don't mind that part. You're a better man than I thought, too, and I might have died anyway. Only I'd be making history now instead of a mess if I hadn't been so damn smart.

LAZEAR. You and me both, Carroll! Damn us both for a pair of incompetent bunglers! When I think of the waste of this! (*But* CARROLL *is laughing.*)

CARROLL. You know I was the first. That's some satisfaction. You can't curse me out of that.

LAZEAR. I didn't mean to curse you.

CARROLL. Some day, when you get a second to back me up and break out in print, find room for me in a footnote, will you?

(AGRAMONTE *enters*.)

AGRAMONTE. Lazear . . . (LAZEAR *turns and fairly runs to him*.)

LAZEAR. News?

AGRAMONTE. (*Holding out a paper*.) His name's on the sick list.

LAZEAR. (*Examining*.) Oh, God bless you, Private Dean! (*He turns back in great exultation*.) Carroll, you're set! We've got your confirmation! (*But* CARROLL *has gone out again*.) Oh . . .

AGRAMONTE. What?

LAZEAR. No. He comes and goes like that. (*Then:*) He was just asking me to . . . (*He stops to control himself. Then:*) I guess I'm tired. (*He sits again*.) Time like this you forget what it's all about. What was it all about? The chase of the carrier of yellow fever. That was it, wasn't it? The chase. (*He smiles*.) I might remember to ask how Dean is.

AGRAMONTE. I don't know.

LAZEAR. You don't know?

AGRAMONTE. I haven't seen him! He isn't in the yellow fever ward. I expect they don't know what's the matter with him.

LAZEAR. If you haven't seen him we don't know ourselves!

AGRAMONTE. Can't we guess?

LAZEAR. I've got to *know!* I can't tell Carroll till I do know!

AGRAMONTE. Can't you show him the sick list with Dean's name on it?

LAZEAR. Carroll wants confirmation!

AGRAMONTE. Tell him you've seen Dean then, and there's no doubt . . .

LAZEAR. I don't want to lie to him if I can help it! Find Dean! He's in this hospital somewhere! Ask where they've put him!

AGRAMONTE. And give the whole show away?

LAZEAR. Who cares what happens now? You've got to see Dean with your own eyes! (AMES *returns carrying, in his hand, the hypodermic needle for* CARROLL'S *injection. He goes to the bed.* LAZEAR *follows. Then:*) Didn't you find any new yellow jack cases?

AMES. No.

59

LAZEAR. Nor hear of any?

AMES. (*Surprised.*) No!

LAZEAR. Go on, Agramonte! (AGRAMONTE *goes, troubled.*) Can I help you?

AMES. Alcohol. (LAZEAR *applies alcohol to* CARROLL'S *arm.*) Hold it. (LAZEAR *holds the arm while* AMES *makes injection.*) Here.

(LAZEAR *takes needle and sets it aside.* AMES *listens with his stethoscope again.* LAZEAR *comes back to bedside.* AMES *looks up. Pause, then:*)

LAZEAR. How long do you give him?

AMES. I don't know. If we could make him fight . . . (MISS BLAKE *has entered.*)

MISS BLAKE. Dr. Ames.

AMES. Yes?

MISS BLAKE. Can you get away to look at a new case? (LAZEAR'S *head comes up.*) It's a soldier they . . .

LAZEAR. (*Almost fainting.*) What's the soldier's name?

MISS BLAKE. (*Consulting a scrap of paper.*) Dean. William H. Troop A. Seventh Cavalry. (LAZEAR'S *eyes close as she continues to* AMES.) And everybody's upset because he insists he hasn't been out of camp for weeks and they're afraid of its breaking out here again and . . .

AMES. (*To* LAZEAR.) Good God!

LAZEAR. (*Low.*) Hadn't you better take a look at him? (AMES *hands* LAZEAR *his stethoscope.*)

AMES. You watch that heart. (*He goes,* MISS BLAKE *following.*)

MISS BLAKE. I'm afraid there's no doubt but it *is* yellow . . .

(*They are gone.* LAZEAR *turns towards* CARROLL.)

LAZEAR. (*Behind his voice that grim pressure which doctors employ to reach through unconsciousness.*) I'll make you fight now, you bloody bonehead! (*He kneels beside bed. His tone is low but shaken with all the force in him.*) You did it after all . . . in spite of yourself . . .

CARROLL. (*As he comes to somewhat.*) I was the first. Remember that . . . I was the first . . .

LAZEAR. (*The pressure increasing as the tone drops in pitch.*) Damn right you were! And nobody's ever going to forget it! . . . We've got your second now! . . . We know now, Carroll! We know! Do you get that! We know! (*Darkness, but not before we have seen the smile on the sick man's face. Then:*)

60

MISS BLAKE. (*Calling frantically through the darkness.*) Dr. Ames! Dr. Ames! (*Light strikes her from behind* AMES *as he enters.*)

AMES. What are you doing up at this time of night?

MISS BLAKE. It's Dr. Lazear . . .

AMES. What's wrong with him?

MISS BLAKE. I don't know! I'm afraid! I went in just now. To make my report on what fine progress Dr. Carroll's making. And he . . . (*Her voice chokes with tears.*) He's very sick, Dr. Ames . . .

AMES. Lazear, too! (*They cross through the darkness, the light increasing to show* LAZEAR *seated at laboratory workbench, haggard and ill, notebooks and sheets of paper scattered before him. The sky remains dead and unlighted.*)

LAZEAR. (*Pushing the words out as he writes.*) I don't deny I bungled Carroll's case, though Dean does seem to have confirmed him. Now they're both out of the woods, I have to confess to you about myself. I can't account for it, but I'm beginning to be afraid . . . (MISS BLAKE *and* AMES *have entered to him.*) Go away. I'm busy.

AMES. She tells me you're under the weather.

LAZEAR. I'd have told you myself if I'd wanted you to know!

AMES. You don't have to tell me. I can see.

LAZEAR. I've got a touch of malaria.

AMES. Sure it isn't the same malaria Carroll had?

LAZEAR. (*Low and stubborn.*) Carroll got yellow jack from our mosquitoes. I haven't taken a bite myself for weeks. Whatever this is, it can't be yellow jack!

AMES. (*Eyeing him sharply.*) The fact remains . . .

MISS BLAKE. Oh, if doctors would only take care of themselves!

(AGRAMONTE *has entered.*)

AGRAMONTE. What's this about Lazear?

AMES. Looks to me very much like . . .

LAZEAR. Don't pay any attention to him, Agramonte!

AGRAMONTE. (*As he sees* LAZEAR.) My God! Have you been trying this again on yourself? You gave me your word . . . (LAZEAR *turns away.*)

LAZEAR. No.

AMES. He's caught it from Carroll, then!

LAZEAR. Don't say that!

61

AGRAMONTE. (*Decisively to* AMES.) No, you get it from a mosquito or not at all!

LAZEAR. That's true! I believe that! I've proved that! (*He has got to his feet in his excitement, but giddiness sits him down again. A pause while* AGRAMONTE *lays an anxious palm on* LAZEAR'S *brow. Then:*)

AGRAMONTE. I don't want to tire you, Lazear. Think back over the last four or five days, though. Hasn't there been one single mosquito that might account . . . I don't mean experimentally. I mean, just in the course of things . . . out of doors . . . ?

LAZEAR. Wouldn't I have noticed?

AGRAMONTE. I hope so! That's why I'm asking you.

LAZEAR. There was one. Yes.

AGRAMONTE. Aha!

LAZEAR. Four or five days back. I was in the wards infecting our mosquitoes and a little stranger 'lighted on my hand. (*Then quickly.*) But it wasn't one of the yellow fever brand!

AGRAMONTE. Are you sure of that?

LAZEAR. Think I don't know these stegomyias by now? It was an ordinary brown one!

AGRAMONTE. You're positive there haven't been any others?

LAZEAR. Positive!

AGRAMONTE. (*Again decisive to* AMES.) Then this can't very well be yellow jack.

AMES. Just the same I wish we could get him to bed.

LAZEAR. I've got work to do. Notes to get up. For Reed when he gets back. (*A pause, then:*)

AMES. He's not getting back tomorrow.

LAZEAR. I know that.

AMES. What's the hurry then?

LAZEAR. Get to hell out of here and leave me alone!!! (MISS BLAKE *gasps.*)

AMES. (*Topping him.*) All I ask is a chance to take care of you!!!

(*Another pause.* LAZEAR *gives up the struggle.*)

LAZEAR. Give me two minutes with Agramonte, you can take all the care you like. (AMES *and* MISS BLAKE *move out of laboratory.* LAZEAR *turns piteously to* AGRAMONTE.) I've done the best I could with these notes. I was just writing Reed a letter. I was going to write my wife. This pair came in. You're the only one of us left on the job now. Will you finish my letter to Reed?

62

AGRAMONTE. Go to bed now!

LAZEAR. I haven't told you what to tell Reed yet. (*His voice drops.*) Warn him to keep Dean's name in the dark. I've called him Private X.Y. in the notes. The truth of that mustn't ever get out. It would bring 'em down like a band of Cossacks.

AGRAMONTE. Is that all?

LAZEAR. No. But I'm not up to thinking of anything more.

AGRAMONTE. What am I to tell Reed about you?

LAZEAR. That's a very neat question! It's a great thing, the scientific life! More ups and downs in it than they know about! But you keep working at it and sooner or later things click into place. The good job well done. It's damn well got to be the good job well done! (*He buries his head in his arms.*)

AGRAMONTE. Ames! (AMES *and* MISS BLAKE *return to laboratory.*) He's worn out. You must get him to bed. (LAZEAR *rises.*)

LAZEAR. All right. I'll go. (*He turns smiling to* AGRAMONTE.) And do you want to know what you can do then, Agramonte? You can take all those notes and all those reports and all those mosquitoes and tell Reed to shove 'em up!

AGRAMONTE. Lazear! What . . . !

LAZEAR. There's nothing in 'em! There's not a damn thing in 'em.

AGRAMONTE. You can't mean that!

LAZEAR. Want to hear a joke? A better joke than the one we had on Carroll?

AGRAMONTE. (*Horrified as he guesses.*) Oh, no, Lazear!

LAZEAR. You've guessed it! I've wrecked our great demonstration, Agramonte! I've shot the whole God damn works to hell! I've gone and got yellow jack without our mosquito!

AGRAMONTE. It isn't possible! How could you!

LAZEAR. (*Again laughing uncontrollably.*) I don't know! I've got it, though! I had it yesterday and I've got it today and my head . . . Oh, my God, my head! (*He collapses forward among the notes and glassware. The two doctors look at him horror-struck.* MISS BLAKE *takes command.*)

MISS BLAKE. We can get him to bed now.

(*Darkness upon a roll of drums. Then the sky takes on the most serene beauty of the light before dawn and light grows where* CARROLL *sits, wasted with recent illness, and* FINLAY *and* GORGAS *stand over him.*)

GORGAS. You must think how easily this might have happened to you. Men can't go against death and not risk death themselves. Pasteur sent Thuillier to Alexandria for the cholera there. Thuillier didn't come back. Lazear won't be the last.

FINLAY. Humanity won't have done asking this sacrifice of his kind for a long time yet. Science won't have done.

CARROLL. His wife's just had another baby. He won't ever see it.

(*Light grows on the screened bed on which* LAZEAR *lies dying.* MISS BLAKE *attends him.* AMES *is just leaving him to approach the other doctors.*)

AMES. Make Carroll go back to bed, Major Gorgas.

CARROLL. How much sleep did he get the nights you thought I was a goner?

GORGAS. He hadn't just been sick. You have.

CARROLL. Lazear's dying! For a lot of God-forsaken halfwits of men and women! Will they ever appreciate what he's done for them? Will they even hear of him?

FINLAY. Neither death nor what he's dying for belong in words.

CARROLL. I haven't got your philosophy, Dr. Finlay. Lazear's the best fellow I've ever known.

GORGAS. And his death is so much waste.

LAZEAR. (*Faintly from behind the screen.*) Waste! Waste!

CARROLL. (*On his feet.*) He heard you! He understood! Lazear!

AMES. Keep your shirt on, Carroll! He's beyond understanding now.

CARROLL. Christ!

GORGAS. Won't you go back to bed?

CARROLL. No.

(AGRAMONTE *enters.*)

AGRAMONTE. Is there any change?

AMES. There won't be before morning. (*He goes behind screen.*)

FINLAY. An admirable young man. There was doom in the look he had. One sees that sometimes. A single task, and at the end, fulfillment.

AGRAMONTE. Fulfillment! Dr. Finlay, don't make this harder to bear than it is already!

CARROLL. I'm with you, Dr. Finlay! I've come around! It was your mosquito that hooked me! There's no other way of explaining me!

FINLAY. This is a time for faith!

AGRAMONTE. Faith in what?

64

FINLAY. In the search at any rate.

AGRAMONTE. What's Reed going to say?

FINLAY. There are worse things than to die seeking. Major Reed will know that.

LAZEAR. (*As before.*) Where's Walter Reed?

CARROLL. (*On his way to* LAZEAR'S *bedside.*) I've got to try once more! I've got to reach him! (CARROLL *goes to* LAZEAR.)

MISS BLAKE. It won't do any good!

CARROLL. It can't do any harm!

AMES. Well, if it's any comfort to you!

CARROLL. It is. (*He bends over foot of cot, speaking at the sick man with that awful clarity doctors use to reach those who are beyond reach.*) Listen, Lazear . . . It's Carroll. . . . Make an effort to get what I'm telling you. . . . Reed's coming back. . . . Do you get that? We've had a cable. . . . He says . . . Tell— Lazear—to—hold—out. . . . Did you hear me? . . . Can you make some sign? . . .

LAZEAR. Waste! Waste!

AGRAMONTE. Good God! (LAZEAR *moves suddenly*.)

LAZEAR. (*His voice rising.*) Waste!

MISS BLAKE. Dr. Ames!

AMES. Stand by!

LAZEAR. (*Struggling to sit up.*) Waste! Waste!! Waste!!! (*He is overcome by* AMES *and* MISS BLAKE.)

AMES. That's better.

GORGAS. He's getting weaker now.

FINLAY. No, Major Gorgas! The stuff of courage doesn't grow weaker! It grows stronger. Stronger and brighter! Until it blinds us! But we do see its flaming sword cut through the veil!

GORGAS. What veil?

FINLAY. (*Pointing.*) Out there, where knowledge hides! (*In the distance the* BUGLER *blows " Reveille."*)

AGRAMONTE. There's " Reveille " !

MISS BLAKE. It's morning already.

LAZEAR. Where's Walter Reed?

(*The characters stand immobile as stage and sky dim to darkness. Then lurid light strikes* BUSCH, MC CLELLAND, O'HARA *and* BRINKERHOF, *huddled together. They speak in hushed whispers.*)

MC CLELLAND. He was still alive at sundown.

O'HARA. When was it he went?

BRINKERHOF. Just now it must have been.

BUSCH. I seen 'em coming back when it was over. Walking and looking at the ground.

O'HARA. A young man and a great one!

BUSCH. I never met him.

BRINKERHOF. I won't forget him but I wish I had something to remember him by.

MC CLELLAND. It's a tough thing to die. It's a tough thing to die like that.

O'HARA. Us medical men have no regrets dying for science.

BRINKERHOF. And for humanity, John.

BUSCH. Humanity. Yeah. That's what us revolutionaries die for.

BRINKERHOF. He died useful just like he lived. It must be a grand thing to be useful.

O'HARA. There's no end to the glory of sacrifice for science!

(*Black-out as light strikes* AGRAMONTE *with the* POST CHAPLAIN.)

AGRAMONTE. (*In intense agitation.*) You call yourself chaplain of this post!

CHAPLAIN. We usually omit the service in such cases.

AGRAMONTE. You're afraid to bury him!

CHAPLAIN. You might find some local clergyman who's had yellow fever.

AGRAMONTE. But I tell you you couldn't catch it from him now!

CHAPLAIN. Can you prove that? (*Black-out as light of the same quality strikes* CARROLL *in violent argument with a* COMMISSARY SERGEANT.)

CARROLL. And you refuse to give us . . .

SERGEANT. I can't issue no post flag for no such purpose!

CARROLL. We've got to have a flag to cover him!

SERGEANT. I'm held responsible for these here stores. I can't issue no flag that's got to be burned after it's used.

CARROLL. I tell you there's no danger!

SERGEANT. I been told different. I can give you a flag to fly over him, but I can't give you no . . . (*Black-out. Light strikes an American flag floating against darkness.*)

COMMAND. (*Off-stage in the darkness.*) Firing squad, atten-SHUN! READY! AIM! FIRE! (*A volley is fired. As the flag is slowly lowered to half-mast the bugle sounds the thin, solemn strains of " Taps." On the last note* REED'S *voice is heard barking sharply through the darkness.*)

REED. Didn't I warn both you and Lazear the night I left you! Unimpeachable workmanship I demanded! And what have you given me? (*Bright daylight shows that the flag has disappeared and that* REED *is striding to and fro in the laboratory, while* CARROLL, AGRAMONTE *and* GORGAS *sit morosely apart.*) You at death's door for no purpose and he dead for less!

CARROLL. Be fair, Reed!

REED. I'm not being unfair! God honor both of you for gallant men!

GORGAS. Reed! You've done enough! The summer's over and the epidemic with it!

REED. There'll be other summers and worse epidemics! There's knowledge and this fact's not yet established!

GORGAS. It's got away from you!

AGRAMONTE. I'm afraid it has.

CARROLL. The hell it has!

REED. Gorgas, I can't let go!

AGRAMONTE. What have you to hang on to?

CARROLL. Let Agramonte go back on this if he wants to, Reed! I'm convinced!

AGRAMONTE. I cannot be romantic about this, Carroll! Scientifically, we have no evidence that Finlay's mosquito played any part either in Lazear's death or in your sickness! And I must agree with Major Gorgas that . . . (*But* BRINKERHOF *has entered.*)

BRINKERHOF. Colonel Tory is here asking for you, Major. (TORY *enters. The entire company rises.* BRINKERHOF *goes.*)

TORY. I welcome your return to Cuba, Major. All my sympathy for your young colleague's death. I call on you to serve a notice on you. The American Public Health Association will hold its annual conference next month. My staff in the Marine Hospital Corps has been invited to report on yellow fever. Since we shall criticize your experiment and you, it seems only fair that you should read what we have to say. (*He proffers a manuscript with a smile of triumph.*) So you may prepare your defense. If you have one.

REED. The usual course would have been to wait for us to make some public assertion. (*He indicates paper.*) This may prevent the continuance of our work.

TORY. I venture to hope it will.

REED. Death has given tragic testimony in our behalf.

TORY. More tragic than conclusive.

REED. I can say no more.

TORY. Major.

REED. Colonel. (*Salutes.* TORY *goes.* REED *turns desperately to* GORGAS.) I need your support desperately now, Gorgas!

GORGAS. Wouldn't you have it if I could give it, Reed? But Lazear did catch yellow fever without your mosquito and you can't keep on in the face of that!

CARROLL. I'm damned if Lazear's death puts a stop to this! (*To* GORGAS.) Lazear was exposed to special dangers, Major! Dangers that don't exist outside of labs! We don't know what he was up to here in our lab! Dissecting mosquitoes! Looking into 'em! And every one of 'em loaded with deadly virus! Any one of a hundred accidents might have happened! A pin prick would have been enough!

GORGAS. You've got to do better than that, Carroll!

CARROLL. What's wrong with that? I believe that! I got yellow jack from a mosquito! You can't account for my case any other way!

REED. There's another case I can't account for either, except . . .

AGRAMONTE.. (*Alarmed.*) Careful, doctor!

REED. We've got to play the ace now, Agramonte. Have you got your Private X.Y. Dean handy? Call him in. Let's see him. I want Major Gorgas to hear me talk to him! (AGRAMONTE *goes to door of laboratory and beckons off-stage.* DEAN *enters and salutes.*) Are you Mr. Dean?

DEAN. Dean. William H. Troop A. Seventh Cavalry.

REED. At ease. You've recently had an attack of yellow fever.

DEAN. I sure have, sir.

REED. We're anxious to learn how you contracted it.

DEAN. I wouldn't mind knowing about that myself!

REED. I have a few questions for you to answer. We'll begin with dates. (*He consults notes.*) We'll begin with the second of September. On that day you were discharged from treatment for a previous illness in the hospital here. And you happened into this laboratory where, at Dr. Lazear's request, you permitted some mosquitoes to bite your arm. (GORGAS *starts.* REED *holds up his hand for silence.*)

DEAN. That's right, sir.

REED. When did you last go into Havana before that?

DEAN. Over the fourth, sir.

REED. August fourth?

DEAN. The Glorious Fourth, sir.

REED. That's two months before you came down with yellow fever. (*A sharp look at* GORGAS.) You can't claim that he caught it that far ahead!

DEAN. What I did catch then was just about as bad.

REED. (*Drily.*) I've seen your record. When did you go into hospital for that?

DEAN. August fifteenth, sir.

REED. How many times did you leave camp between July fourth and the fifteenth of August?

DEAN. Just once, sir.

REED. In six weeks, only once?

DEAN. Me and four others rode five horses a mile and a half down to the beach and back.

REED. And you stayed in hospital till the day in the laboratory. September second.

DEAN. That's right, sir.

REED. Now it was four days later that you reported sick with yellow fever. (*Full blast.*) How about those four days?

DEAN. They had me working around camp, sir.

REED. (*Another glance at* GORGAS, *then he produces a ten dollar bill from his pocketbook.*) Mr. Dean, I'll give you ten dollars if you'll admit that you went some place where you might have been exposed to yellow fever during those four days.

DEAN. I tell you I never left camp, Major! I couldn't get leave!

REED. You went without leave, Mr. Dean.

DEAN. Major, I swear to God!

REED. You needn't be afraid of my telling on you. I give you my word I won't. Now, didn't you leave camp once during those four days? If only for an hour, didn't you? You could use ten dollars.

DEAN. No, sir. I didn't! So I can't take the money!

REED. Thank you, Mr. Dean. That's all I need to know.

DEAN. You asked me a lot of questions about me having yellow jack. How about finding the guy that give it to me? (*An embarrassed pause, then:*)

REED. Here! (*He produces another bill.*) Here's twenty dollars. That's twice as good as ten. There are no strings tied to it.

DEAN (*Taking it.*) Say! Gee! Thanks! (*He remembers himself.*) Thank you, Major!

REED. Thank you, Mr. Dean. (*He turns triumphantly to* GORGAS.)

GORGAS. May I put one question to Mr. Dean?

REED. Discretion, please!

GORGAS. I understand. (*To* DEAN.) Who was present in this laboratory on the day you let those mosquitoes bite you?

DEAN. (*Pointing to* AGRAMONTE.) That gentleman there, and him that died—Dr. Lazear—and an elderly gentleman.

AGRAMONTE. Dr. Finlay.

GORGAS. Thank you. (*To* REED.) That's all.

REED. We won't detain you any longer, Mr. Dean. (*Salutes.* DEAN *goes.*)

GORGAS. (*Embarrassment.*) I know what it is to hope, Reed, but I can't accept a soldier's word in lieu of demonstration.

REED. (*Frantic.*) Surely that story of his indicates something!

GORGAS. If you could substantiate every word he said you'd still have to admit he was in this lab that day with three doctors any one of whom might have carried the infection from Carroll's bedside! If he's all the defense you have against Tory, I'm sorry for you!

AGRAMONTE. He's perfectly right. We haven't any defense.

CARROLL. Do we sit tight, then, and let Tory do his worst?

REED. No! I believe our mosquitoes have the real deadly stuff in 'em! I believe Lazear really did find the catch before he died! In spite of his death and Gorgas's doubts I believe it!

GORGAS. You've all gone off your heads over this!

REED. I can see I'm in no shape to convince you, Gorgas! But, by God, we *have* got enough to take to Leonard Wood! (*Both* CARROLL *and* AGRAMONTE *are on their feet in great excitement.*)

CARROLL. Wood!

REED. He's our last chance, Carroll!

AGRAMONTE. What can Wood do for us?

REED. I can't tell you that! I can only tell you what I shall ask him for!

GORGAS. And what will that be?

REED. (*Full blast.*) Facilities for a fool-proof demonstration of this mosquito! The full power of his governor-generalship behind us! Ten thousand dollars for operating expenses! An isolation camp where we can experiment under ideal conditions! And his leave to call for volunteers to experiment on! I think the time has come for that at last! (*Sensation.*)

QUARTET. (*Softly in the distance.*)

> "You're in the army now!
> You're not behind the plow!
> You son of a bitch,
> You'll never get rich,
> You're in the army now!"

CARROLL. So we fall back on the army after all!

REED. As soldiers should, Carroll! As soldiers should! (*The light dims, concentrating on the four officers.*)

GORGAS. Do you think Wood will even consider that?

REED. I don't know, Gorgas. All I know is: Lazear and Carroll showed the way! And I know this will give the army a new kind of hero! Do you think Leonard Wood won't see that? (*Darkness, the* QUARTET *swelling. At the same time light strikes* AMES, *where he is talking to a sergeant.*)

AMES. Understand now, Sergeant, General Wood doesn't want any pressure brought. Just let it leak out. Keep it going all over camp. I don't know why any healthy kid should volunteer, but three hundred's a lot of money to a soldier. (*Then night sky and the* QUARTET *is singing "There'll Be a Hot Time in the Old Town Tonight" and* SOLDIERS *in a seemingly interminable line of silhouettes are trooping along the horizon. They are all talking and gesticulating excitedly.*)

SOLDIERS. Now, what was that again? . . . Just what I heard. Three hundred dollars' compensation for volunteers . . . Volunteers to catch yellow jack and die of it? . . . I'm telling you what I heard . . . They got a nerve! . . . It's the God-damnedest thing I ever heard of! . . . I *don't* think! . . . *I'm* not crazy! . . . Three hundred dollars! . . . I'm only telling you what they told me! . . . How did you hear about it? . . . General Wood fixed it up with Major Reed . . . He told Dr. Carroll, who told Dr. Ames . . . I heard him telling one of our sergeants . . . Ain't you boys heard how the Major . . . You're crazy! . . . I'm only telling you what they told me! . . . Would you take a chance on it? . . . For three hundred dollars? It's a pile of money! . . . Not for me! Not for mine! . . . Three hundred dollars! I wouldn't for three thousand! . . . No, I've been lucky enough to come through this far! . . . I ain't taking no more chances neither . . . I'll keep my health, if the Major's got no objection! . . . What do they take soldiers for anyway! . . .

71

What do they think they're doing! . . . Catch yellow jack . . .
Die of yellow jack! . . . What for? . . . Three hundred dollars!
. . . To advance science! . . . And benefit humanity! . . . Good
God Almighty! . . . Ain't soldiers humanity! . . . (*Four* SOL-
DIERS *have drifted down from the line of passing silhouettes and
now as light grows upon the steps we see that they are* BUSCH,
MC CLELLAND, O'HARA *and* BRINKERHOF *and that* MISS BLAKE *is
seated in the midst of them.*)

MISS BLAKE. You can't say it hasn't given camp something to talk
about!

MC CLELLAND. Well, as long as they don't do nothing but talk!

BRINKERHOF. Are you sure talking's all there is to do?

MC CLELLAND. It's all for any man with any sense.

BUSCH. I wouldn't be so sure of that, Mac.

O'HARA. I'm tempted! Holy God, I'm tempted!

MC CLELLAND. Still, three hundred dollars is a lot of money.

BRINKERHOF. A man couldn't do a thing like this for money.

MC CLELLAND. What would you do it for?

BRINKERHOF. There's patriotism.

MC CLELLAND. That's what landed us in the army!

BRINKERHOF. I ain't said I'd do it. For argument, though, and not
committing myself, if Dr. Lazear was still alive, I'd consider doing
it for him on personal grounds.

MC CLELLAND. I wouldn't do it on personal grounds for God
Almighty!

O'HARA. Are you on personal grounds with God Almighty?

BRINKERHOF. Never bring religion into an argument.

BUSCH. It's the very sum of money I been praying for! Jesus,
maybe it's a hunk of muzal!

MISS BLAKE. The Major said: " Tell the boys this gives them a
real chance to advance medical science and benefit humanity."

BRINKERHOF. Medical science and humanity ain't bad reasons.

MC CLELLAND. What's medical science ever done for me?

BRINKERHOF. You been to the dentist, ain't you? That was medical
science.

MC CLELLAND. Am I supposed to catch yellow jack for dentists?

BRINKERHOF. Well, don't ask me what humanity's done for you
or I'll ask you where you'd be without it!

BUSCH. It's an awful way to earn money, but I could use it!

MC CLELLAND. I got nothing against the financial offer. All my objections are to the yellow jack.

BUSCHE. It's an awful risk. I wonder if it's worth it!

MC CLELLAND. There's an old army rule I wouldn't forget. Keep your mouth shut and your bowels open and never volunteer.

BUSCH. If this was economics I could make up my mind, but it ain't, and I can't get no guidance out of Karl Marx!

MISS BLAKE. "Tell them they'll be giving the army a new kind of hero," the Major said.

O'HARA. Glory be to God, 'tis the heroic side appeals to the Irish always, as I said to myself when I made up my mind I'd do it!

MISS BLAKE. You did make up your mind?

O'HARA. Would you think a man of my type could resist volunteering?

MISS BLAKE. I knew they'd get one of you!

O'HARA. You should have known it'ud be me, Miss Blake! And I'm with John Brinkerhof! I'll only do it free, I said!

MISS BLAKE. That's beautiful!

O'HARA. But that height of nobility, naturally as I come by it, is not practical. As I soon realized when I thought how well I could use this sum of money for my medical training which, as you well know, is my life's ambition. So I made up my mind I'd accept the payment.

MISS BLAKE. And why not?

O'HARA. Would you believe it, the heroic side got in my way and stopped me! What a noble start I'd be getting in my profession, I thought, if I can say later: "Yes, I am that same John O'Hara who gave his life that mankind might be preserved from yellow fever!" There was an uplifting notion for you! With that in my mind I went running to the Major.

MISS BLAKE. I knew he'd get one of you!

O'HARA. Oh, no man could have held me back if I hadn't thought still another thought in the nick of time. "If I do give my life," I said to myself, "it may be noble, but will it be a start?"

BUSCH. It's a thing any radical could go into and not be ashamed of, only I got to have more time on it.

MISS BLAKE. Won't the Major get a single volunteer?

BRINKERHOF. I wouldn't know.

MISS BLAKE. I want him to get one.

O'HARA. Don't be using your sex to shame us into this!

MISS BLAKE. I'm talking to Mr. Brinkerhof now. To Mr. Brinkerhof, who wants to stay on in the army. Drill. Ten, maybe twenty

73

years of drill. Then another war. And more lives thrown away. Then drill again. Then a pension and the old soldiers' home. If that's all being a soldier comes to!

BRINKERHOF. It ain't much.

MISS BLAKE. Now, maybe for the first time since armies began, soldiers are given a chance to do good, not harm. To make the world better, not worse, as a place to live in. (*They listen hypnotized*, O'HARA *rising slowly to his feet.*) You'd get well! We'd take care of you! Don't be afraid!

BRINKERHOF. But I *am* afraid.

MISS BLAKE. That makes it all the braver!

BRINKERHOF. I wouldn't do it for money!

MISS BLAKE. For your sergeancy then!

BRINKERHOF. That'd be just as bad.

MISS BLAKE. For science and humanity!

BRINKERHOF. Oh, I'd never be up to anything like that!

MISS BLAKE. Choose your own reason!

BRINKERHOF. There'd be a lot of satisfaction in it.

MISS BLAKE. Indeed there would!

BRINKERHOF. No! Just to me, I mean!

MISS BLAKE. But that's enough!

BRINKERHOF. I ain't committed myself! I only said, for the sake of argument . . .

MISS BLAKE. "If one, only one, of our boys will step forward," the Major said, "he'll make this reach and touch the heart of the world and the world will weep and have faith in this!"

O'HARA. By God, I'll do it for the hell of it! (*A glad cry from* MISS BLAKE. *"Call to Quarters" sounds.*)

MC CLELLAND. For Christ's sake, O'Hara!

O'HARA. Will you come with me, John?

BUSCH. Don't be in a hurry, Brinkie!

O'HARA. Will you come with me!

BRINKERHOF. Where?

O'HARA. To the Major!

BRINKERHOF. Now?

O'HARA. Before I have time to change my mind again!

BUSCH. It's a God damn gallery play! All he wants is to be a hero!

BRINKERHOF. I don't know that I'm cut out for a hero, John!

O'HARA. Will the Major know that? Would any man with the sense of science in him look a gift hero in the teeth!

MC CLELLAND. You're crazy, O'Hara!

74

O'HARA. I am not crazy! This is the better side of my nature rising up, as it's sure to do in the end with the Irish! (*To* BRINKERHOF.) Are you coming or do I have to drag you!

BRINKERHOF. Oh, I'm coming, John! I'm coming!

BUSCH. Stop him!

MC CLELLAND. (*To* MISS BLAKE.) You talked him into this!

MISS BLAKE. Thank God if I did!

MC CLELLAND. You're responsible if they . . .

MISS BLAKE. I can't help that! I can't help wanting them to . . .

(*But* O'HARA *has already pulled* BRINKERHOF *to his feet, turned him about and dragged him over below where* REED *is waiting in the upper shadow alone.* REED *sees them and, while the others look on breathless, comes down to them and returns their salutes.*)

REED. Did you want something, Mr. O'Hara?

O'HARA. We've come to volunteer, sir.

BRINKERHOF. The both of us, sir. For the experiment. (BUSCH *makes as though to follow them, then draws back to* MC CLELLAND *and the pair stand together frightened.* MISS BLAKE *remains motionless in her exultation.* REED *smiles, then a deep breath, and:*)

REED. You know the risk?

O'HARA. Yes, sir, we know, all right.

REED. You've heard what the compensation is?

BRINKERHOF. Yes, sir, we've heard. Only . . . (*He catches* O'HARA'S *eye.*)

O'HARA. (*Drawing himself up in the manner of a schoolboy speaking a valedictory oration.*) We're volunteering in the interests of science, sir.

BRINKERHOF. (*Same manner.*) And for the benefit of humanity.

O'HARA. And the only condition on which we volunteer . . .

BRINKERHOF. Is that we receive no compensation, sir. (*Pause.*)

REED. Gentlemen, I salute you. (*He does.* O'HARA *and* BRINKERHOF *are covered with confusion. Darkness, but immediately the regimental band bursts full blast into " The Stars and Stripes Forever " and* CARROLL *is standing in light in front of the laboratory screen, a carnival barker selling it to the universe.*)

CARROLL. Did you hear that, folks! Did you see it! We're off and nobody can stop us now! We've got heroes to answer 'em with now! And Wood's given us everything else we needed! Backing, dough, isolation camp! This is it, folks! Camp Lazear we call it! Ideal conditions! No mosquitoes here we don't bring with us in

75

test tubes! And we're going to show you the God-damnedest demonstration that's ever been! (*Light strikes the tent below, where* BRINKERHOF *and* O'HARA *sit solemnly on their bunks, stripped to the waist.*) O'Hara and Brinkerhof are in that tent this minute! Two weeks they've been there, where not a thing could get at 'em! So you couldn't ask for more perfect subjects than they'll be when they step out to take their bites today! And they'll get yellow jack, no fear of that! But they're only the half of this show! (*Light strikes a crude windowless wooden shack above.*) Do you see that shack? Reed isn't satisfied just to nail the mosquito and stop there! Not Reed! He's going to show 'em that nature's got things fixed so you can't catch yellow jack any way *but* from the mosquito! Never you mind how Lazear caught it! This is what happens in nature, not in labs! And Reed's thought up the God-damnedest scheme! (*Daylight begins slowly to spread over the stage and what has been a bustle in the darkness is now seen to be caused by a horde of American* SOLDIERS.) He calls that shack "the dirty house"! And it's dirty, all right! He's packed it full of every stinking by-product of this disease that ought to spread it around if anything could and he's got two more soldiers . . . (*A particularly bright light picks out* BUSCH *and* MC CLELLAND *standing close together, frightened and wishing they had not come.*) . . . to sleep nights in there for three weeks! They're going to sleep in the unaired, undisinfected and unwashed bedding and night shirts men have died in, on pillows and mattresses soaked with fever sweat and black vomit! And wouldn't it take a God-fearing son of a bitch of a workman like Reed to do a thing like that to a couple of kids? But if we keep the mosquitoes out of that shack, the chances are good—and they're damned good, folks!—that this second pair doesn't catch yellow jack! And that ought to show our fellow doctors and scientists they've been wrong in everything they ever thought about this! By God, if this job doesn't make medical history . . .

BUSCH. I wonder if we were right about volunteering.

MC CLELLAND. Why?

BUSCH. Once you get in you don't get out.

MC CLELLAND. I thought of that, too. (*He calls.*) O'Hara!

(O'HARA *emerges from tent.*)

O'HARA. Come out, John, and see what's putting itself forward where it's not wanted. (BRINKERHOF *follows him out.*)

MC CLELLAND. Who says we're not wanted and who don't want us?

O'HARA. Too many heroes leave none outstanding which is not in agreement with the Irish ideal!

BRINKERHOF. I'm sure the Major wants all that'll come, John.

O'HARA. Will you think before you speak, John, or not speak at all? (*To* MC CLELLAND.) What brings you here, whom I last heard scorning the very idea, and did you refuse compensation like the two of us or are you selling your bodies like a couple of whores?

MC CLELLAND. We're taking all the compensation we can get on account we got no use for gallery plays!

BUSCH. And me doing this for the wherewithal to further the radical movement puts me above any bourgeois hero and what's heroes amount to and who wants to be one?

O'HARA. Heroes amount to the inspiration of mankind! And the difference between compensation and none leaves John and me our superiority! (*The* BAND *concludes the Sousa march.* REED *has entered above, followed by* AGRAMONTE, *who carries the mosquitoes in the usual gauze-capped tubes.*)

A SERGEANT. AttenSHUN!

AGRAMONTE. Are you ready, Reed? (*Complete silence, then:*)

REED. I'm ready. Carroll, call the roll.

CARROLL. O'Hara. Brinkerhof. Busch. McClelland. (*Each* SOLDIER *answers up.*)

REED. Now, then, Mr. Busch and Mr. McClelland, you'll take up your residence in the dirty house. (BUSCH *and* MC CLELLAND *move slowly up towards the shack. They open door and spring back in horror.*)

MC CLELLAND. Christ Almighty! (BUSCH *turns to* REED *with a sickly grin.*)

BUSCH. I never knew anything could stink like that!

MC CLELLAND. (*The same state of mind.*) Me neither. But it's too late to back down now. (BUSCH *replies with a little Jewish gesture of resignation which sums up two thousand years of making the best of things.*)

BUSCH. I'll pull the blankets out. You make up the bunks. (*He goes into the shack.*)

MC CLELLAND. They just closed the Paris Exposition! I read about it in the papers. You won't never read about this. Nobody could write how this smells! Take a good look, heroes! (*He goes into the house.*)

REED. Sergeant, close the door. (SERGEANT *closes and padlocks door.* REED *turns to* O'HARA *and* BRINKERHOF.) Are you ready, Brinkerhof and O'Hara?

BRINKERHOF. We had a good sleep, a good breakfast and a sterile bath. I don't know what more we got coming to us.

O'HARA. Unless somebody would be after taking our pictures?

BRINKERHOF. Why would you want your picture taken, John?

O'HARA. I like a bit of a send-off, John, but it doesn't matter.

REED. I'll give you a send-off. (*He turns to* AGRAMONTE.) Will you give me the mosquitoes, Agramonte? (AGRAMONTE *steps towards* REED *with the test tubes. A longer roll of drums off-stage. Darkness. Then light grows within the lower tent and the sky is tropical night once more.* BUSCH *and* MC CLELLAND *sit smoking in front of the wooden shack.* O'HARA *lounges in the opening of the lower tent, within which* BRINKERHOF *sits on a cot in the act of taking his temperature. A* SERGEANT *stands apart.*)

SERGEANT. Five minutes more, boys. Then recess is over.

BUSCH. Ain't the Major coming to tell us good night?

SERGEANT. Don't he always come to tell you good night?

BUSCH. He don't pay no attention to the two of us. (*Indicating* BRINKERHOF *and* O'HARA.) He ain't interested only in those two guys. (SERGEANT *goes. A pause.*)

O'HARA. Being a hero should be quickly over and on to the glory that comes after.

MC CLELLAND. Will you listen to all that quiet!

BUSCH. I heard it before and I didn't like it. They'd ought to have give us a bugler out here.

MC CLELLAND I never expected this to be this way. This was a hell of a Thanksgiving Day!

BUSCH. I ain't complaining. I'm putting on weight living in that stink.

O'HARA. (*To* BRINKERHOF.) Will you take that thermometer out of your mouth, John!

BRINKERHOF. I'm hot.

O'HARA. It's a cold night with a wintry dampness in it the way you could see your breath if you troubled to blow it!

MC CLELLAND. O'Hara!

O'HARA. What is it?

MC CLELLAND. How are you feeling?

O'HARA. I'm feeling fine.

BUSCH. How's Brinkerhof feeling?

O'HARA. He feels better than me.

BRINKERHOF. I don't feel well, John! I got vertigo.

O'HARA. If you don't feel right it's your willful imagination! If you felt bad I'd feel worse than you! Do you think it's friendly to try stealing a march on me? We started on this together and we'll finish together or not finish at all!

BRINKERHOF. This is the night of the fourth day. The Major said things ought to begin to happen the fourth day.

O'HARA. For the last time I tell you, if you've got a fever you're no friend of mine!

MC CLELLAND. Quit scrapping, O'Hara!

BUSCH. We'll all be scrapping before we get out of this. (*A pause, then:*)

O'HARA. Likely there'll nothing come of this in the end. Likely we'll wait here for two days or three, then go back to be the laughing stock of the barracks.

MC CLELLAND. That has one drawback you ain't thought of, O'Hara. If nothing don't come of this for neither of you, then the Major's mosquitoes ain't as dangerous as he thought. And if they ain't, the stink inside there may not be so safe!

BUSCH. For God's sake, don't say that!

O'HARA. Are you afraid?

MC CLELLAND. Why wouldn't he be? We been sitting inside there all afternoon. Waiting to hear the ambulance take one or both of you off to the hospital! When they let us out to eat supper, there both of you was as big as life and twice as healthy! Can you imagine how that made us feel! Looks like Busch and me may be the heroes who catch yellow jack!

O'HARA. The cowardice of those remarks sounds highly suitable on your tongue, McClelland, and it coated with the biliousness of beer!

BUSCH. It's only half-wits ain't afraid of danger.

MC CLELLAND. I hope that's some consolation to you. (*General irritability.* BRINKERHOF *has risen to close the tent flap.*)

O'HARA. What are you after doing with that tent flap?

BRINKERHOF. I'm cold.

O'HARA. Two minutes ago the fever was burning you up!

BRINKERHOF. I got a chill now. My ears is roaring and my teeth is chattering and my head . . .

O'HARA. You'll not give yourself yellow jack ahead of me, sucking thermometers one minute and chattering your jaws together the next! This was agreed to be both of us or neither! (*The* SERGEANT *returns.*)

SERGEANT. Pipe down! (*Silence, then he continues to* O'HARA.) Major ordered the ambulance to stand by on the chance that either you or Brinkerhof might need it.

O'HARA. You can tell the ambulance to go to bed.

SERGEANT. All right. Lights out.

BUSCH. (*Rises and goes to shack.*) Either the stink inside is weakening or we're getting used to it. (*Opening door of shack, he stops on the threshold.*)

MC CLELLAND. No, she ain't weakened much.

BUSCH. The fresh air makes her seem worse than she is!

MC CLELLAND. Take a deep breath outside. (*He goes in.*)

BUSCH. (*To* O'HARA *and* BRINKERHOF.) We'll feel safer if the both of you die before morning! (*He fills his lungs and follows* MC CLELLAND *into shack, closing the door. The* SERGEANT *padlocks door on outside and goes. In the meanwhile:*)

BRINKERHOF. You been hard on me, John. You know I wouldn't take no advantage of you if I could help it. (*Removing his shoes, he shudders again as with a chill and looks up.*) You wouldn't like to speak some Shakespeare for me? You usually like to when there's no one around. If you said your favorite lines from Julius Cæsar, they might put heart in me. (*Another shudder of chill comes over him. He looks uneasily towards* O'HARA, *then reaches stealthily for the thermometer, shakes it, sticks it back in his mouth and turns away so that he will not be observed. In the meanwhile:*)

O'HARA.

> " Cowards die many times before their death;
> The valiant never taste of death but once.
> Of all the wonders that I yet have heard,
> It seems most strange to me that men should fear,
> Seeing that death, a necessary end,
> Will come when it will come."

BRINKERHOF. (*His diction obstructed by thermometer.*) Thank you, John. (O'HARA *turns furious.*)

O'HARA. Are you at that thing again! Give it to me! I'll smash it to atoms!

BRINKERHOF. (*Defending it.*) No, John, don't break it.

O'HARA. I want no more of your treachery! (*He secures thermometer.*)

BRINKERHOF. Don't break it, John! Look for yourself! See if I ain't got something wrong with me! (*O'HARA looks scornfully. Then bends to look more closely under the lamp. Then:*)

O'HARA. Holy God! (*He hands thermometer back to BRINKERHOF, who reads it. They look at one another, BRINKERHOF nodding with a sickly smile.*)

BRINKERHOF. It'd go higher if I gave it time.

O'HARA. And me as fit as a fiddler's bitch in heat! (*He feels his brows, his pulse, and strikes his chest despairingly.*) What ails you, O'Hara, that you let others get ahead of you? Here, give me that thing back! (*He snatches thermometer from BRINKERHOF's mouth and puts it into his own.*)

BRINKERHOF. Could I ask you to go down to the ambulance and tell them? (*Pause, as O'HARA takes thermometer out of his mouth, is disappointed, puts it back to suck it harder than ever.*) Could I ask you, John? (*Staring uncomprehendingly, O'HARA again removes thermometer from his mouth. Then he turns suddenly and runs out, shouting as he goes:*)

O'HARA. Ambulance! Ambulance! Ambulance!

MC CLELLAND. (*From within shack.*) What the hell! What are you yelling about out there?

BUSCH. They got it, Mac! They got it!

MC CLELLAND. Which one of 'em's got it? (*Door of shack is rattled from within as they beat upon it.*) Is it you, Brinkerhof?

BUSCH. For God's sake!

MC CLELLAND. Answer up!

BUSCH. Let us out of here! Let us out! (*The turmoil continues, with BRINKERHOF on his feet, frightened and swaying dizzily. Then darkness and immediately upon it the QUARTET is singing "Good-bye, My Blue Bell." The chorus through once and daylight strikes BRINKERHOF in bed. FINLAY and GORGAS bend over him, subjecting him to an intense and meticulous examination. MISS BLAKE stands apart to one side, REED to the other. The examination continues in pantomime over the music. Apart and somewhat above on the side opposite BRINKERHOF's bed, CARROLL and AGRAMONTE are waiting, AGRAMONTE pacing restlessly to and fro.*)

AGRAMONTE. (*After a pause.*) Will they never finish their examination?

CARROLL. You're taking this harder than Reed is.

81

AGRAMONTE. I feel for Reed. This is Reed's moment. Everything hangs on what Gorgas says.

CARROLL. Whatever Gorgas says, that's a real case of genuine yellow jack.

AGRAMONTE. But the world will listen to what Gorgas says. (FINLAY *straightens and turns to* GORGAS.)

FINLAY. Well, Major Gorgas?

GORGAS. I'll give my opinion when I've seen the records.

REED. Miss Blake has the records for you. Suppose you take them aside to look them over. I don't want you to tire the boy out.

(GORGAS *and* FINLAY *see* REED'S *point and go to* MISS BLAKE.)

GORGAS. Yes, I expect we were being a bit inhuman.

FINLAY. That's one of the drawbacks of experiment, Major Gorgas. (*They have crossed to* MISS BLAKE, *who hands them each a file of the record. They sit to study them in silence while she looks on and* CARROLL *and* AGRAMONTE *watch from above.* REED *has gone to* BRINKERHOF'S *bedside and stands looking down on him.*)

REED. That was part of the game, Brinkerhof. An essential part from my point of view. I hope you didn't mind it too much.

BRINKERHOF. I wouldn't feel up to minding anything, doctor.

REED. It's a bad sickness, I know that. We got your case at the beginning, though, so you're going to be all right. Don't worry.

BRINKERHOF. I wouldn't feel up to worrying, either. (REED'S *hand is on the boy's forehead.*)

REED. They tell me you didn't drink the champagne I sent you.

BRINKERHOF. Do I have to drink it, sir?

REED. It might make you feel less sick at your stomach.

BRINKERHOF. I ain't used to it and I didn't care for it. (REED *smiles, then:*)

REED. My wife's just sent me a fine fruit cake. I'm saving it for you. For your Christmas dinner. We'll try to have you on your feet by then. So you can get sick all over again. Not for science, though. Just for the fun of it. Nothing else we can do for you now? (*A pause.* BRINKERHOF *manages to lift his head a little. Then:*)

BRINKERHOF. Why was it, sir, yellow jack took me and give O'Hara the go-by?

REED. (*Surprised.*) I don't know, Brinkerhof. Some men seem to be born immune to some diseases.

82

BRINKERHOF. Could a man be immune one time and catch it another?

REED. It's possible. We don't know much about immunity.

BRINKERHOF. John O'Hara he's quite a friend of mine, sir. You just asked me what more you could do for me. John set his heart on getting this disease for the start it'd give him practicing medicine. It's likely the only start he'll ever get. Would you give John another chance at it, sir?

REED. It's hard for me to say no to you, Brinkerhof. I'm afraid O'Hara's a waste of time for my purposes. I can't afford to break our record of success. I'll do what I can to help him with his medical studies. But I wish you'd ask me for something else now.

(BRINKERHOF *sinks back.*)

BRINKERHOF. Give John my best. Ask him not to be angry with me if he can help it.

REED. I'll do that much. (*But* GORGAS, *going through file, has come to the fever chart.*)

GORGAS. (*Low and quick.*) A hundred and three and six tenths last night. Dropped again, though, at six this morning and again at eight.

FINLAY. You've noticed the granular casts in the urine, I hope?

(REED *goes toward them.*)

GORGAS. Oh, yes.

FINLAY. The eyes were beautifully jaundiced today, too.

GORGAS. (*To* MISS BLAKE.) How about the gums?

MISS BLAKE. A little bleeding.

FINLAY. Headache and nausea still troublesome, though?

MISS BLAKE. He's very uncomfortable.

FINLAY. Splendid! I should defer to the Major's diagnosis, but I can't think of a symptom the boy's omitted! It's beautiful! Beautiful! The fourth day of his sickness, too! (*Then, to* REED.) And how long did you say between the bite and the first symptom?

REED. Three days, nine and a half hours.

FINLAY. Nineteen years for me! Three days, nine and a half hours for Major Reed! (*He is pumping* REED's *hand.*) I conceived a truth! You delivered it into life! Together we have added to the world's arsenal of knowledge!

GORGAS. You promised you'd make me eat my doubts, Reed.

Didn't know eating doubts could be such a pleasure! Damned if this isn't an impressive moment! I'm going out after this mosquito now. And after that, Panama! You've made the Panama Canal possible now! May I? (*He holds out his hand.*)

REED. (*Sternly.*) If that boy's convinced you, Gorgas, that he did get the infection from the mosquito and if those other two, healthy as ever in the filth of that dirty house, have shown you the disease cannot in nature be contracted except from the mosquito, then you may! But if you have any shadow of reservation on either point . . . (AMES *has entered hastily to second cot.*)

AMES. You certainly are knocking 'em over out at that camp, Major! Will you fix up this cot, Miss Blake? (MISS BLAKE *goes to prepare cot.*)

CARROLL. What do you mean?

AGRAMONTE. You haven't got another case from out there!

REED. Not Busch or McClelland!

(*Together.*)

AGRAMONTE. They couldn't have caught it in the dirty house!

REED. There hasn't been a mosquito near that pair . . .

CARROLL. That'd wreck things worse than Lazear's death did, my God!

FINLAY. Oh, no, no, no! Not just at the moment when we . . .

GORGAS. Good Lord! Well, it goes to show you never . . .

(*All talking together in their dismay, the three members of the* COMMISSION *have left* FINLAY *and* GORGAS *and hurried towards* AMES. *Before they can reach him, however, two* STRETCHER BEARERS *have carried a stretcher in and the recumbent form upon it belongs to* O'HARA.)

REED. (*Climax.*) O'Hara!

O'HARA. (*Feeble but triumphant.*) Good afternoon to you, doctor.

REED. But this man hasn't got yellow fever, Ames!

AMES. Oh, yes, he has!

CARROLL. (*To* O'HARA.) But, God damn it, you should have come down four days ago!

REED. That's true. O'Hara! How . . . ?

O'HARA. Have you never heard, Major, how it's the human element that still baffles you men of science?

84

AGRAMONTE. That is no answer!

REED. (*Shaking with excitement.*) Do you know how you got it?

O'HARA. You weren't out at camp the day after they took Brinkerhof away.

REED. No.

O'HARA. You should have left those mosquitoes of yours locked up! (*Sensation.* MISS BLAKE *is shocked,* REED *stunned.*)

BRINKERHOF. (*Feeble, but delighted.*) Hooray! (*The light focuses sharply down upon* O'HARA.)

O'HARA. Now science and humanity become one in the person of Johnny O'Hara! And no shadow of gain for him but his own satisfaction, and only the hell and vanity of that! (*Darkness, and the* QUARTET *strikes into " The Old Folks at Home." Then the sky is night once more and the foreground bare and dark and the only illumination of the setting is within the laboratory, where* REED, CARROLL *and* AGRAMONTE *are dimly visible.* REED *comes out of laboratory, the other two following.*)

REED. Well, Carroll, the job's done and the doubts and discouragements are memories now. And the last microscope's packed and we've closed the door of our Cuban laboratory. And our dirty house has made us a fine bonfire and grass can grow once more where Brinkerhof and O'Hara pitched their tent. And none of the boys seem much the worse for wear and we're going home. I could wish we were taking Lazear home with us. I could wish that you were coming, Agramonte.

AGRAMONTE. No, doctor. I am Cuban born. I must stay in Cuba.

(BRINKERHOF *enters and salutes.*)

REED. Yes, Mr. Brinkerhof?

BRINKERHOF. The rig you ordered to take you down to the transport's ready, sir, whenever you are.

REED. Are you and O'Hara ready to sail with us?

BRINKERHOF. Yes, sir. We're ready, sir. O'Hara he's still a bit weak in the knees. He's resting down there on the pile of baggage.

(REED *turns smiling up the stair, but* CARROLL *is after him.*)

CARROLL. Let's not go, Chief! Let's stay and finish things! It can't be far from here to vaccine and cure! Are you with me, Chief?

REED. No, Carroll, I'm not with you. A man does what he has to do and is tired. (*They are all four silhouettes now against the*

85

sky.) I see the struggles and tragedies ahead. (*In the distance the African tom-tom begins to throb faintly.*)

AGRAMONTE. Yes, Carroll. For the men who will follow after us and carry on the chase in the years to come. In Ecuador and Mexico and Brazil. And in that vast reservoir of African jungle whence this thing came, where it will persist. . . . (*The tom-tom swells suddenly and* REED *lifts his hand as though to silence* AGRAMONTE *so that he may listen to the future, and the four, motionless, recede into the past. At the same time, indeed already through* AGRAMONTE'S *last words,* STACKPOOLE *has entered below to a faint glow of light, thoughtful and detached, and is standing motionless. Simultaneously* HARKNESS *has entered to a brighter light on the other side below.*)

HARKNESS. Lagos, West Africa. September 19th, 1927. Dr. Adrian Stokes died here of yellow fever this afternoon after an illness of three days and a few hours. We cannot say how he contracted the disease. It is certain that no infected mosquito had bitten him. In that, his death recalls the death of Dr. Lazear in Havana, in 1900. It would appear that yellow fever laboratories are filled with dangers hitherto unrealized. Stokes continued directing our work from his bed, insisting that his blood be taken for injection into monkeys and that mosquitoes be fed on him for infection. His work ceased only as he sank into the final coma. Due to the mildness of yellow fever among African natives, Stokes felt that we should never be able positively to demonstrate that we had given his monkeys the real thing until we had seen white man and monkey both dead of the same infection and side by side on the autopsy table. . . . (*The light on* HARKNESS *dies to a glow, leaving him as motionless as* REED *and his group above and behind. Simultaneously it increases on the waiting* STACKPOOLE.) We have seen that now in the autopsy just performed on Stokes himself.

STACKPOOLE. London. September 23rd, 1929. Conclusion of experiment on monkeys one hundred and seventeen and one hundred and fifty-five. Summary of record. These two monkeys were vaccinated on January 12th last, according to the principle established for dog distemper by Laidlaw and Dunkin, namely, a combination of immune blood with active virus. Being still in good health on April 12th following, the animals were on that date injected with a fatal dose of active virus, to which they showed no reaction. No conclusion was drawn from this single success, however, and both animals were held, still in good health, until September 12th, when one hundred thousand fatal doses of virus were administered to each. The fact that the health of these animals remains good on this, the tenth day following so severe a test, indicates . . . (*He corrects himself.*) . . . would indicate . . . (*He corrects himself again.*) No, damn it, *does* indicate the establishment of at least a principle of vaccination against yellow fever. Reed took the disease from mosquito to man. Stokes took it from man to monkey. Now we shall be taking it from monkey back to man. (*The* CHORUS *strikes full force and full volume into the refrain of " There'll Be a Hot Time in the Old Town To-night " and there is a distant sound of* SOLDIERS *marching and the light goes into darkness and the play is ended.*)

Successful Plays For Amateurs

Junior Miss

Stage Door

Arsenic and Old Lace

Seven Sisters

Sweet Charity

The Man Who Came to Dinner

George Washington Slept Here

Cuckoos on the Hearth

(Most of the titles above are available everywhere, but in order to make certain of availability write direct to the Dramatists Play Service, Inc.)

SEND FOR FREE DESCRIPTIVE
CATALOGUE

JUST PUBLISHED IN A SPECIAL ACTING VERSION

STAGE DOOR

Play in 3 acts by Edna Ferber and George S. Kaufman. This unusual play was produced at the Music Box Theatre, New York, by Sam Harris, where it ran for a season, and then toured the country with immense success. It was recently released as a picture, featuring Katharine Hepburn and Ginger Rogers. *Stage Door* is offered to universities and Little Theatres and to certain high schools, junior colleges, and private schools in the belief that more ambitious and advanced groups are willing and anxious to use on occasion a finer and somewhat more adult type of play than is chosen by the average.

The story tells of a large group of young and ambitious girls who have come to New York to study acting and find jobs in the theatre. The scene is Mrs. Orcutt's *Footlights' Club,* a boarding house for girls, where all the hopes and ambitions of sixteen young women are revealed to us in scenes of keen observation and for the most part entertaining comedy. Contrasted with this background are the pathetic cases of the girl without talent and the elderly actress whose days are over; but the central plot has to do with the dynamic and courageous Terry Randall, who through thick and thin fights her way against discouragement and poverty to a position in the theatre where we are sure she will conquer. One of her fellow-aspirants gives up in despair, one gets married, and one goes into the pictures, but Terry, with the help of idealistic David Kingsley, sticks to her guns.

Rarely have we had a play in our modern theatre which offered so many rôles for young women, or so sympathetically dramatized the ambitions of young womanhood of today. Color and contrast are offered to the scenes involving the young women by the characters of Mattie, the colored maid; Frank, her husband; a few young men callers, a movie magnate and young Keith Burgess, the Left Wing playwright who " goes Hollywood."

Most of the action takes place in the living-room, but there is one scene in one of the bedrooms, a small set which can easily be put inside the larger one. The printed text of the play is a literal transcript of the acting prompt copy, and includes pictures of the sets, full stage directions, property plots and ground plans.

Play in 3 acts. 11 men; 21 women (16 young women). 2 interior settings.

Paper-bound books, 75c. Production fee $25.00 a performance.

★ The Last Word in Make-Up

A Practical Illustrated Handbook

By Dr. Rudolph Liszt

An up-to-the-minute work for all who use make-up on the stage, in the classroom, in the home, on the street, and in the photographer's studio. Compact, direct, and easy to understand. It is preeminently practical and may be used by drama students and teachers alike. It is one of the most completely illustrated works ever issued, containing 44 half-tone photographs and over 80 original sketches made by the author.

Among the subjects fully treated, in graded form, from primary to advanced, are:

THEATRICAL MAKE-UP

MAKE-UP FOR STRAIGHT AND COLOR
  PHOTOGRAPHY

MAKE-UP FOR MOTION PICTURES

SOCIETY AND STREET MAKE-UP

TECHNICOLOR MAKE-UP

TELEVISION MAKE-UP

Though these are all covered in the book, it is primarily a work for those engaged in nonprofessional theater work.

The Last Word in Make-Up is the only book on the subject with a complete chart offering at a glance instructions as to the exact means of making up hundreds of parts. This is easily arranged in alphabetical order, beginning with "Arab" and ending with "Zulu."

"Dr. Liszt can achieve any effect he wants, and give it the air of authority."—*Boston Transcript.*

"Unique and authoritative . . . Contents presented with true showmanship."—*Film Daily*, New York.

Cloth-bound volume, illustrated with 44 photographs and over 80 drawings.

Price, $1.65